Walking on the Way

Hans-Ruedi Weber

Walking on the Way

Biblical Signposts

WCC Publications, Geneva

Cover design: Rob Lucas
Cover illustration: See outside back cover

ISBN 2-8254-1357-7

© 2002, WCC Publications, World Council of Churches
150 route de Ferney, P.O. Box 2100
1211 Geneva 2, Switzerland
Web site: http://www.wcc-coe.org

No. 97 in the Risk Book Series

Printed in Switzerland

Contents

Preface

In the autumn of life I was asked to write about the key Bible texts that have shaped me. I found it difficult to make a choice after half a century of biblical study, writing and teaching on different continents, because working with people of different cultures has brought so many passages alive. Rather than making an arbitrary selection, it seemed wiser to group my reflections around the great feasts that have been celebrated by Christians since the early centuries. This would allow me to go back once again to Jesus and the gospels. In order to get a clearer focus I have based these studies mainly on the testimonies of Luke.

The ecclesiastical year usually starts with the season of Advent and the birth of Jesus, although the feasts of Christmas and Epiphany appeared relatively late in the worship of the church. According to both the biblical evidence and to earliest church practice, it is better to begin with the Passion and Easter season (Chapters 2 and 3), followed by Pentecost (Chapter 4). But Christian life does not consist only of this great sequence of primary feasts; it also includes long stretches of day-to-day living where it is difficult to maintain our faith. Before setting out on his public ministry and his journey to the cross Jesus himself spent some 30 years in that everyday world. That, therefore, must become our starting point (Chapter 1). And when we have reached Pentecost the waiting for the great Advent (Chapter 5) continues, the waiting for the new heaven and the new earth. The appendix offers suggestions on planning participatory Bible studies for those who want not simply to read these reflections but to explore with others some of the key texts.

Living within the rhythm of the ecclesiastical year is a good discipline to maintain faith. It gives a depth to the cycle of the civic year. There is, though, the danger that the meaning of the great feasts can stagnate and become imprisoned in dogma and fixed liturgies. The ecclesiastical year then becomes a closed circle. I find it increasingly hard to go on remembering, year after year, the great events and affirmations of biblical faith in the same way. Therefore I like to think of the cycle of feasts not as a circle but as a spiral that may open up new, surprising layers of meaning. Moreover, the great feasts and the stretches between them are strongly linked. The cross is not only for Good Friday and the hallelujah is not only for Easter. Pentecost was originally not a day but a whole season, deeply connected with all life on this earth. Advent embraces all of time and creation.

The following reflections are written partly for myself, to express both my hope and deep conviction of faith and some of my uncertainties and doubts. My primary aim is to be an advocate for the biblical texts. This means the close reading of what the Bible actually says, whether or not we like it, whether or not it fits our philosophy of life and accords with our confessional tradition. I simply want to let Jesus and the evangelists speak to my readers. I will offer no novel theories, hypotheses or profound new theologies, but a straightforward teaching of biblical faith, seen through the lens of Luke's testimonies and my own limitations.

Those familiar with technical and computer language can find the words of the Bible difficult to understand. What the evangelists write has not only an informative but also a strongly evocative function. The theologies of the Bible, the biblical speaking and thinking about God, come to us most often in the form of theo-poetry, which aims not to define and delimit but to open up meanings. Therefore Jesus taught about the kingdom of God by telling parables and his prophetic gestures often spoke more strongly than his words. This is why, for many years, I have tried to combine biblical interpretation through historical and literary text analysis with learning from artists' interpretations using images, symbols, movements and sounds. Throughout the centuries musicians, painters, sculptors, architects, weavers, actors and, more recently, film-makers have been the major popular interpreters of the Bible

In recent years tapestry weaving has become one of my hobbies. It is a meditative art. As the hands form patterns with the weft and the warp, I can ruminate on central biblical themes that have become important in my life. In between the preparatory reading for and the writing of the following reflections I have tried to conceive and weave five small symbolic tapestries, one each for discipleship, Good Friday, Easter, Pentecost and Advent. The many hours of sitting before the loom became very meaningful and have helped my understanding.

These meditations are dedicated to Jan Kok. He was the one who challenged me to take up writing again. He courageously walked on the Way and has now passed through the mysterious door of death. I am grateful to Ineke, who introduced me to the craft of weaving, and to a host of scholars, linguists, historians and exegetes. Only one will be mentioned here: Luke, the author of the third gospel and of Acts, through whose testimony the life of Jesus and of the early Christians comes alive.

H.R.W.

1. A Way to Follow?

"Are you he who is to come, or shall we look for another?" An imprisoned prophet, John the Baptist, sent two of his followers to ask Jesus this question and throughout the centuries Christian believers have secretly or openly asked the same thing. It is often in my mind too. The watershed of history in which we live today affects all continents, creating new hopes and shattering old convictions. Can Jesus be a guide in this fascinating and bewildering time of worldwide communication and increased meeting of cultures and faiths? Those who ask this question are seriously attempting to be involved as Christians in the affairs of this world. Before over-confidently answering "yes" or settling down in a luke-warm tolerant half-belief, it is good to go back to the sources of Christian faith.

The testimony of the evangelists

Mark, Matthew, Luke and John wrote some three to six decades after Jesus died. Meanwhile the apostle Paul had already dictated his passionate letters to the churches outside Palestine. What we find in the gospels of the sayings and acts of Jesus comes to us only through what the earliest witnesses remembered and transmitted, what they and the evangelists themselves interpreted for their own situation. We can no longer go back directly to the "historical" Jesus. Every attempt to do so, including what is written in this book, tends to project onto him and his time the questions, convictions and prejudices of our own. Nevertheless, I would like to meet *him*, not simply the "Lucan Jesus" or the "Johannine Jesus" of the New Testament scholars or the Jesus of the Orthodox, Roman Catholic or Protestant dogmatic teachers. I trust that if we take time to study, with intellectual honesty and prayer, the testimonies of the evangelists, *he* will address us in and through later interpretations.

Throughout these reflections Luke will be our main witness: he will act as our eyes. Testifying about Jesus, he starts in Jerusalem, the centre of the Jewish-Palestinian world, and ends in Rome, the capital of the empire. Luke lets us walk with the first disciples on the dusty village roads of Galilee, then takes us through the crucial weeks in Jerusalem which are the focus of what Christians have since celebrated at Good Friday, Easter and Pentecost. Then Luke helps us to accompany the apostles Peter and Paul on the highways and seaways of the Mediterranean world to reach its thriving cosmopolitan cities and enter into the Greek-Roman culture of that time. No wonder he needed two volumes – the gospel and the Acts – for his testimony. With so many journeys to describe, one can understand why "the Way" – the "way of the Lord" and the "way of salvation" – became one of Luke's favoured descriptions of the meaning of Christian faith and life. Whether the author was the "beloved physician" who accompanied the apostle Paul on part of his missionary journeys remains a much disputed question, but his purpose for writing is clear: he wants to show readers that Way and encourage them to walk according to it.

When Jesus was a young man

The evangelists tell us little about the boyhood of Jesus of Nazareth and his growth to maturity, but one thing is certain: he was a Jew, not a Christian. This obvious truth continues to surprise, even to shock, Christian believers. It is good, though, to start with this fact. The only gospel notice about the boy Jesus, the scene of the 12-year-old on the temple premises of Jerusalem (Luke 2:41-52), both presents this information and qualifies it at the same time. How much of this account is based on reports of what actually happened can no longer be ascertained. Clearly, Luke wrote it not simply as a biographical anecdote but almost as a parable for what the Way is all about.

The boy Jesus sits in the circle of the Jewish teachers (not "at the feet of" these venerable rabbis as later Paul sat at the feet of the rabbi Gamaliel). He listens and asks questions. "And all who heard him were amazed at his understanding and his answers." According to Jewish law, Jesus was not yet an adult, nor had he, as far as we know, had any rabbinical training. Moreover, he came from outlying Galilee, from Nazareth, a village never even mentioned in the Jewish scriptures. Yet he showed astonishing insight and wisdom. When his worried parents finally find their missing boy they are not so favourably impressed. They cannot understand his behaviour and Mary reprimands him: "Look, your father and I have been searching you in great anxiety". He responds: "Why were you searching for me? Did you not know that I must be in my Father's house?" (The original Greek text has only "in my Father's": the word "realm" or "enterprise" could be added.) Here, as there will be throughout the gospel, there is a conflict between two different understandings of doing God's will and of fatherhood. For the first time we meet here also a key term that characterizes the whole of Jesus's way: a divine "must". Then, and for some two decades, Jesus fitted into the pattern of Jewish life. He went home with his parents, obedient, growing in wisdom and years and in divine and human favour. Though she did not yet understand, Mary treasured all that happened in her heart.

This scene helps us to guess how Jesus grew up. He came from a pious family, which followed the requirements of the Jewish law. They went up to Jerusalem each year for the celebration of the Passover feast. From the childhood stories we know that, as a little boy, Jesus had been circumcized. Each day, therefore, he bore the covenant-sign on his body. According to the Mosaic Law, his parents had presented him as a firstborn male to God in the temple. Later Luke tells us that, "as was his custom", Jesus went to the synagogue on the sabbath day. It remains uncertain whether Nazareth already had a synagogue building at that time, but it must be remembered that the term "synagogue" referred primarily to an assembly of people, not an actual structure. In small villages the synagogue may have met for prayer and teaching in the market place or in private homes. From several gospel texts we can also assume that Jesus grew up in a family with other children. He worked with his father as a craftsman: the Greek term usually translated as "carpenter" could equally well refer to another craft, such as stone cutting (Nazareth had stone quarries) or weaving (Galilee was well known for its linen), but it was most likely linked with building.

The writings of the Jewish historian Josephus, archaeological discoveries and, indirectly, the parables of Jesus give us glimpses of daily life in Galilee during the early first century AD. Except in the mountainous north, the land was fertile and densely populated. Besides fishing and subsistence farming some of the produce, such as olives and linen, was exported. The Jewish villages were occupied mainly by farmers and artisans, together with landless and often unemployed labourers. The cities had an ethnically more mixed population, already strongly influenced by the Greek-Roman culture. This was especially the case in Sepphoris, the old capital of Galilee, and in Tiberias, founded in AD 23 as a new capital. For over half a century the region was under indirect Roman rule.

After the death of Herod the Great in 4 BC one of his sons, Herod Antipas, became the tetrarch of both Galilee and Perea for 43 years. Educated at the imperial court in Rome, he had imbibed Greek-Roman culture and, like his father, was keen on building new cities. This, of course, meant heavy taxation and increasing urbanization of the originally rural Galilee. In the gospels Herod Antipas does not have a good name: he is the one who allowed John the Baptist be imprisoned and beheaded. Jesus once called him a "fox" (Luke 13:32). Only Luke reports that Herod was in Jerusalem during the trial of Jesus. Pilate asked him to interrogate the troublesome Galilean miracle worker, but Jesus refused to answer and "that same day Herod and Pilate became friends with each other" (Luke 23:6-12). Nevertheless, Herod showed more sensitivity to Jewish customs and religion than did most of the Roman procurators in Judea which, together with Samaria, had been under direct Roman rule since AD 6.

Galilee is generally known as a hearth of Jewish resistance against Rome. Only a few years after Jesus's birth uproar against Roman taxation and a struggle for Jewish-Galilean identity started in Sepphoris, a mere 7 kilometres from Nazareth. The rebellion, led by Judas the Galilean (see Acts 5:37), was quickly crushed by the Roman army. The city was destroyed (it was later magnificently rebuilt by Herod Antipas) and its population sold into slavery. Some decades later Galilee became deeply involved in the first Jewish war (AD 66-70). In Jesus's life-time, however, it was a comparatively peaceful area. Nothing certain is known about the social condition and political convictions of Jesus's parents. Galilean artisans in villages probably also owned or rented a little piece of land for subsistence farming. Was this the case for Joseph? How did he and the young Jesus react to the rebellion of Judas the Galilean? Did they have affinities with one of the various Jewish "parties" of that time? Or did they identify more with the poor "people of the land" whose whole energy was concentrated on the struggle for survival? We do not know.

The Bible of Jesus
A little more can be guessed about what we might call the religious education of the young Jesus. In pious Jewish families the whole of daily life was a continuing learning process. The main teachers were the parents, and especially the father for boys from adulthood (13 years) onwards. Jesus probably participated in daily family prayers and, as a young adult, went to synagogue worship. It is unlikely that, during his boyhood, a school was attached to the synagogue assembly of his village. According to later Jewish sources, it was only Josua ben-Gamala (high priest in AD 63-64) who ordered that, in every town outside Jerusalem, teachers should be appointed to educate children from the age of six or seven. What Jesus knew about his national and religious background he learned in the family, by participation in the cycle of Jewish feasts and during pilgrimages to Jerusalem. Learning took place through memorization and loud recitation rather than through silent reading; through movement, rituals and symbols rather than through sitting in a classroom.

It is instructive to remember what the "Bible" looked like for the young Jesus. It obviously appeared quite different from our bound paper book with its printed text. Then, it was a collection of scrolls of parchment containing handwritten copies of parts of the Hebrew scriptures. The synagogue kept these precious scrolls. With the exception of the Torah (Genesis to Deuteronomy), not all synagogue assemblies owned the scrolls of all the prophets and the other writings that are now bundled together in what Christians call the Old Testament. At the time of Jesus the collection remained open-ended because the list (the canon) of the authoritative Hebrew scriptures was fixed only after AD 70.

We can assume that each week in the synagogue assembly Jesus heard a passage from the Torah and from a prophet. These lessons in Hebrew were usually freely translated into the common language of the people, Aramaic. Each day Jesus recited the "Hear Israel" *(Shema Israel)*, confessing the one God with the words of Deuteronomy 6:4-7, 11:13-21 and Numbers 15:37-41. And possibly, for the morning prayers, he also bound the *tefillin* on his forehead and on the inner side of his left upper arm. This consisted of ribbons onto which were fixed two small black leather boxes containing parchments of four key texts: Exodus 13:1-10, 13:11-16 and the first two of the Shema *(see Fig. 1)*. These passages were thus literally placed near the brain and the heart and they were certainly deeply imprinted in the boy's memory and mind. He felt very much part of that special people of Israel, freed from slavery in Egypt and called in a special covenant relationship to love, obey and serve God. At Passover celebrations, like all believing Jews, he became a contemporary participant in the exodus event. When asked about the reason for the unleavened bread, he was taught to say: "It is because of what the Lord did for *me* when *I* came out of Egypt" (Ex. 13:8ff.). Besides these great texts from the Torah Jesus of course knew by heart the stories of the patriarchs, many proverbs and many of the psalms, chanted at feasts and during pilgrimages.

Two prophets

This ordinary Jewish life as a boy and a young adult suddenly came to an end. When Jesus was about 30 years old, he

Fig. 1: Tefellin and prayer shawl

left family, home and trade and became an itinerant healer, teacher and prophet. He went to be baptized by John the Baptist, then called a group of disciples whom he asked to leave everything and to share his wandering life. This was not totally unheard of. Some 150 years earlier other Jewish men had left their ordinary daily life and followed a great "teacher of righteousness" into the Jewish desert to form the Qumran community. There also were itinerant philosophers who must have visited the Hellenistic cities in Galilee. Many in first-century Palestine felt a sense of urgency, expecting a catastrophic end to history or the sudden breakthrough of God's direct reign on earth. Various groups hoped for the coming of differently understood prophetic and messianic figures. For instance, during the decades before Jesus's birth, the Qumranites expected the coming of the prophet Elijah as the predecessor of two Messiahs, the priestly one of Aaron and the royal, military one of Israel. In that context the appearance of neither John the Baptist nor Jesus of Nazareth was considered unique.

In the childhood stories of Luke's gospel John the Baptist and Jesus are set side by side: two announcements of their birth, complemented by the meeting of the two expectant mothers; then two accounts of their birth, circumcision, naming and future greatness, complemented by their growth in spirit and wisdom. In this juxtaposition the precedence of Jesus is consistently emphasized. The narratives and hymns of these first two chapters form the link between the promises of the Hebrew scriptures with the life of Jesus. They also relate strongly to the book of Acts. What the early Christians later discovered gradually under the guidance of the Spirit is already anticipated in the childhood stories. Therefore high titles are assigned to Jesus, titles that he never applied to himself before his death and resurrection: "Saviour", "Messiah", "Son of God". Clearly, although Jesus had a very strong sense of being in intimate communion with God (Luke 2:49, 10:22), he avoided such high titles, filled with meanings that did not correspond with the direction he had to take. After the first two chapters of Luke's gospel Jesus was generally addressed as a "teacher" or "master" and considered to be a "prophet". When speaking about himself Jesus often used the expression "Son of man". In apocalyptic sayings this recalls the heavenly figure of a coming ruler and judge similar to the one who appears in Daniel 7:13ff. More often "Son of man" refers simply to a human being; it can replace the "I". When used with active verbs it usually points to Jesus' spiritual authority in, for instance, forgiving sins or transgressing sabbath laws. When used with passive verbs it refers to Jesus as the suffering servant and the persecuted prophet.

Rabbinical teachers used to say that since the deaths of Haggai, Zechariah and Malachi, the last prophets, the Holy Spirit had ceased in Israel. The heavens were closed, though one could still hear an echo of God's voice. To walk according to God's will, Jewish believers had to rely on the guidance of the Torah and the counsel of the sages. Luke, however, testified that there had been a new breakthrough of God's Spirit. Two new prophets arose. If a reporter could have interviewed Luke and the disciples of John and Jesus, he might have received answers like those quoted on *Worksheet A* (compare and use the parallel texts on pp. 92-93).

Both John and Jesus had a strong sense of urgency. They acted and spoke as if the end of history had arrived. Both "announced good news". The verb used does not simply mean to preach or teach a message but to come running and publicly proclaim unheard of and ultimately joyful news. Both addressed themselves to the crowds, but their origins, places of appearance and ways of action were not the same (notice their different main areas of work areas on the map, p. 10). Above all, there was a notable difference in the "good news" they came to bring.

The Baptist came from a village near Jerusalem. In Judea, and especially in the priestly family of his parents, life centred on the Jerusalem temple. Like Samson and Samuel, John, from childhood, was totally dedicated to God's service (Judg. 13; 1 Sam. 1; Luke 1:15). He therefore fasted, drank no wine and lived an ascetic life in the desert lands of the exodus story where, long before, Elisha had received the mantle of the prophet Elijah. It was there that "the word of God came upon" him, just as it had for the great Old Testament prophets. He then moved to the River Jordan where he gathered an astonishing variety of people around him.

John came to proclaim three related messages:

1. The whole land and its inhabitants had become unclean and therefore God's judgment was imminent. Neither the claim to be Abraham's children nor daily and annual purification sacrifices in the temple could avert the coming judgment. A new rite must be performed. Formerly only converts to Judaism were baptized. Now John initiated a baptism for Jews as a seal for repentance and forgiveness of sins. This baptism had to take place in the Jordan through which, long before, Joshua and a few Israelite tribes had entered the promised land. The new rite was to symbolize that a repentant and renewed people of God could once again enter the Holy Land.

10

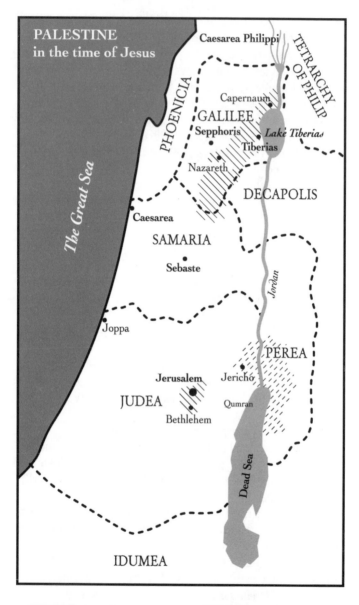

PALESTINE
in the time of Jesus

Caesarea Philippi

TETRARCHY OF PHILIP

PHOENICIA

Capernaum

GALILEE

Sepphoris

Lake Tiberias

Tiberias

Nazareth

DECAPOLIS

Caesarea

SAMARIA

Sebaste

Jordan

Joppa

PEREA

Jerusalem

Jericho

JUDEA

Qumran

Bethlehem

The Great Sea

Dead Sea

IDUMEA

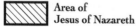 Area of
Jesus of Nazareth

 Area of
John the Baptist

2. The repentance must become visible in decisions and deeds. Based on the teaching of the Torah and on prophetic exhortations, the Baptist gave practical advice for daily living and work during the time that remained before the end.

3. Above all, John testified that he had come only as the predecessor of a mightier one: the judge who would bring the decisive turn of ages. He would cleanse the people and the land by the Spirit and fire of God. The two Old Testament passages quoted in this connection are significant. Isaiah 40:3-5 is the beginning of prophecies uttered by an unknown prophet in the Babylonian exile, announcing a new exodus, leading to salvation and liberation. The "way of the Lord" mentioned there refers to God's way, but the Baptist applied this prophecy to the mighty one who was to come. The passage from Malachi 3:1, with which Jesus characterized the Baptist, refers to the cleansing of God's people through the final judgment and the coming of the revived Elijah who would initiate a new age.

John's message was a severe one. Later, when he was in prison, what he heard about Jesus worried him and gave rise to doubts. Jesus somehow did not fit the profile of the one whose coming he had announced. Therefore he sent his disciples to ask, "Are you the one who is to come?" We might well ask whether what Luke tells us about Jesus before his crucifixion fits our own expectations today.

The prophet of God's kingdom

Jesus was a Galilean. According to Luke, he spent most of his two- or three-year public ministry in a very limited area: a quadrangle of villages and townships north and west of the lake of Tiberias, not more than 10 kilometres wide and 20 kilometres long. He never seems to have entered the cities of Sepphoris and Tiberias, though he visited some villages in Samaria. Jerusalem was three days' travel to the south and Luke does not report that he went there before his final journey to the cross.

Having been baptized, perhaps after being for a time a disciple of John the Baptist, Jesus returned to Galilee, filled with the power of the Spirit. He became the itinerant prophet of God's kingdom. (For many today, that term has male and autocratic overtones, but it will be used here with the proviso that it must be filled with the same meaning Jesus himself gave to it.) The last chapter of these reflections will concentrate on the coming kingdom; here it is enough to note that for Jesus and the Jews of his time God's kingdom was nothing less than a new heaven and a new earth. What Jesus announced can be visualized as in *Figure 2*. From creation onwards, world history and the journey of the Israelites has

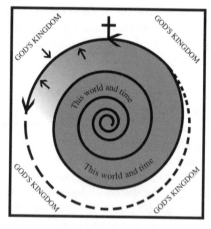

Fig. 2

run towards the end in a spiral movement. Now the frontier between this world and time and God's kingdom has been reached and the remaining time moves on the circumference, the edge between the old and the new heaven and earth. Nobody knows when or how soon the kingdom will appear.

The prophecy of Jesus took the double form of teaching, mainly through parables, and of healing by exorcisms and forgiveness. He left home and became an itinerant prophet in Galilee, his way finally leading also to Judea and Jerusalem. When he was a boy it had been a divine "must" to be in his father's house and realm. Now, as an adult, it became a divine "must" to "proclaim the good news of the kingdom of God" all over the land. When the Baptist addressed the crowd, he began with "You brood of vipers!", but Jesus's message announced that "Your sins are forgiven!" and "Blessed are you who are poor!" True, there also was a "Woe to you!", but the main emphasis lay not on judgment but on healing. In answer to John's question he responded neither with a "yes" or a "no", nor with a messianic title or a doctrine about himself. He simply told the Baptist's disciples, "Go and tell John what you have seen and heard: the blind receive their sight, the lame walk, the lepers are cleansed, the deaf hear, the dead are raised, the poor have good news brought to them. And blessed is anyone who takes no offence at me" (7:22-23, with many allusions to prophecies of the book of Isaiah).

All that Jesus did and taught shows a clear preference for and sympathy with the poor, the lost and despised. His way of being with them and for them was not the violent one of Judas the Galilean and the later Jewish resistance fighters. He answered the power of violence with the power of love and a willingness to become the victim. Jesus was radical but he was not a fanatic. When he said that the healthy need no physician and that he did not come to call the righteous, he meant it. For him as a Jew the righteous, the just, were a reality. He knew the story of rebellion in Genesis 3 and he was aware of the evil inclination in all human beings. Yet no doctrine of original sin obscured for him the knowledge that God's creation is essentially good and that all humans are created in God's image. Of the seven passages in Luke's gospel where people are called "righteous/just" only two have the pejorative meaning of hypocritical self-righteousness. Jesus was not one to spoil the joy in life. When the tax collector Levi, whom he had just called into discipleship, organized a feast, Jesus joined in, eating and drinking. Even in the emergency situation of God's kingdom being at hand Jesus did not appear to worry and hurry. He had time and was available for children, outcast women and the ill. When he had restored their health and joy in life he usually did not ask them to become his followers.

This healing, conciliatory and at times festive atmosphere is only half of the picture. Exorcism means a struggle with demonic powers and, moreover, Jesus soon came into conflict with the Jewish teachers of the law. Interpreting the whole of the Torah and the prophets through the prism of the double command of loving God and loving one's neighbour, he was free, for love's sake, to transgress the sabbath laws. Claiming authority to forgive sins, he became a threat to the temple authorities in Jerusalem. Jesus went to the temple to pray and teach, but it is never reported that he participated in purification sacrifices. It was not any messianic claim he made for himself which led to his trial and crucifixion. Rather, it was his announcement of the imminent destruction of the temple and his powerful presence and proclamation which created a threat.

Those called by Jesus into discipleship had to participate in his struggle and his empathy with the poor and needy. Sociologically speaking, this fellowship of disciples was an impossible group. In a time and society of deep divisions and fanatic separatism, Jesus created a new fellowship. It included fishermen from Galilee as well as Judas the Zealot, who was probably a former anti-Roman resistance fighter. The tax collector Levi/Matthew, who collaborated with the Roman rule, became part of the group, as did Mary, Martha and other women who received him and followed him. Later even the learned Pharisee Saul/Paul, formerly a fierce persecutor of the Way, joined the company.

Trying to visualize this call into discipleship, I made a tapestry with footprints in the desert, but the Japanese artist Takeji Asano has created a much more telling image in the woodcut "Strangers and Exiles on the Earth" *(Plate I)*. It expresses well what discipleship implies: walking against the ungodly currents that dominate their time. In this way the disciples responded to the extraordinary call, "Follow me!" Jesus asked them to deny themselves and to carry their cross each day. They had to leave homes and families and jobs. They were asked to give priority to God's kingdom even over the most sacred duties: "Let the dead bury their own dead." It is not clear whether such demands are made of all disciples. We know for certain that the 12, the first to be called

Plate I: "Strangers and Exiles on the Earth", woodcut by Takeji Asano, Japan, 20th century

"apostles", shared his itinerant, unprotected life, sent out "to proclaim the kingdom of God and to heal" (Luke 9:2). Others, like the 70 mentioned later in Luke's gospel, perhaps became such itinerant messengers only temporarily. There were still others, the "crowd of disciples", who believed in him but probably stayed in their village and continued their daily work. Often they would become hosts for Jesus and his followers. They formed part of the Jesus movement, expecting the breakthrough of God's kingdom very soon, if not in their life-time. Together with Jesus, they lived on the edge between this world and God's kingdom.

Walking on the edge

Luke knew better than the other evangelists that things did not develop as Jesus had expected. Two or three generations had already followed the Way, and God's kingdom had not yet come. In the Acts Luke tells how Peter, Paul and others continued Jesus's itinerant ministry. He also reports that the followers of Jesus in Jerusalem attempted to share all their possessions. Yet the physiognomy of the Jesus movement was changing. Most of those who were now called "Christians" continued their ordinary daily life and work. They gathered for worship and mutual support in local congregations and many no longer immediately expected the end of the world they knew. Apostles and their helpers continued to spread the gospel and helped new congregations to grow, mainly in the cities of the Roman empire. Local leaders emerged, presbyters for leading the life of Christian communities in their towns.

Fully aware of this development, Luke did not water down what Jesus had taught and demanded. He recorded the radical exigencies of the call to discipleship although he knew that, outside the rural society of Palestine, the growing number of Christians could not lead such an itinerant life with no possessions, no family and no home. There still were wandering Christian prophets in Luke's time, but they became an exception. The earliest known catechism and church order, the Didache (from before AD 150), already manifests the uneasiness of the new church leaders about such travelling teachers and prophets. It regulates the hospitality that local churches may or not give to them (*Didache*, 11-13).

* * *

Meanwhile almost 2000 years have passed and the kingdom of God has not yet come. John the Baptist's enquiry remains valid: Is it really possible to walk on the edge between this world/time and God's kingdom? Many of our contemporaries never ask this question because they have never heard of Jesus or because they have dismissed him. Luke and the early Christians confessed that Jesus is indeed the one for whose coming they and the nations have hoped. For me, often a doubting Thomas, the question still stands. I feel ill at ease with the many ways by which Christians throughout the centuries have "solved" the great tension between what Jesus was and what he taught during his earthly life and what churches usually show and teach in human society.

I have no better "solution" and can offer only some personal convictions:

- What Jesus was, did and taught before his death and resurrection remains an existential challenge and provocation. This Jesus of history must not be swallowed up by later doctrines about Christ. Of course the story continues. The next chapters will reflect on Jesus's crucifixion, resurrection and the gift of the Spirit.

- Jesus' manifestation and proclamation of God's coming kingdom is concerned with what is to happen on this earth and at the close of this time. The gospel forbids us to escape into a purely other-worldly or merely individualistic spirituality. It also calls us to political, economic and ecological responsibility.

- The kingdom of God in Jesus's life and teaching comes out of Jewish apocalyptic expectations. It is, however, more than a concept or myth that can be exchanged or demythologized without betraying the gospel. We must attempt to wait and work for it in our own apocalyptic time.

- For their faith and faithfulness Christians need something like a third type of apostolic succession. This must complement that of bishops and church leaders (the *magisterium*) and that of the teachers of faith (the *magisters*). Also needed is a succession of "fools for Jesus' sake", living on the edge of this world and the kingdom. Throughout history these people have been given to us inside and outside the established churches. They constitute an odd company. Some of them are found among martyrs, among nuns, monks and pioneer missionaries. Others we meet among social reformers and revolutionaries, among women and men with a dream.

For the rest of us, who cannot follow the call of Jesus in such a radical way, it is salutary to remember again and again what lies at the heart of Jesus's message and life: "The kingdom of God is near" (Luke 21:31). At times I like to go walking with a biblical text. Learning it by heart, keeping it constantly in mind, I try at the same time to be sensitive to what I see, hear and spontaneously remember. How does this text relate to the child, the busy crowd, the polluted water or the publicity posters I see? What is its relation to the traffic noise I hear or the waiting task I recall? All these make claims on us and often overwhelm us. How does the world around us interpret the text? And how does the text interpret the world and convert my thinking and decision-making?

Go walking in this way with the text: "The kingdom of God is near."

2. The Just One on the Cross

Look at the fragment of Coptic tapestry on the cover of this book. It was woven probably more than 1000 years ago in Egypt. Throughout the centuries the dry desert climate kept the form and beautiful colours almost intact. Did the Coptic Christian weaver in fact want to portray a cross? And, if so, how did he interpret that symbol while working at his loom? Do you know how such a woven fabric is made, how it stays together and remains flexible even after centuries? If you are not acquainted with the ancient craft of weaving, find a torn piece of an old cloth and begin to take it apart, thread by thread. Weavers will tell you there are many different ways of making such hand-woven textiles: some are very simple, just interlinking the threads, whereas others use complicated combinations and knots. Whatever the manner of production, each such fabric consists of thousands of hidden crosses where the weft and the warp intersect, making it flexible and keeping the whole together.

As soon as we put on clothes we are surrounded by a host of invisible crosses. When we become aware of this fact and begin to reflect on it, it becomes a strong parable for what weaves people and society together and enables movement and life. Whatever our belief or unbelief, all of us unconsciously carry the cross, the symbol that has become the major signpost of the Way, in our daily lives.

The sign of the cross

The cross appears as a symbol in almost every culture and religion. Often it points to the sun or the four cardinal directions of the cosmos. For most of our contemporaries it recalls suffering, sorrow and death. Nobody who has ever seen the rows and rows of white crosses in military cemeteries on the battlefields of the 20th century will ever forget them. In everyday life the sign has lost much of its symbolic, evocative power. It simply became an ornament, a piece of jewellery.

The last letter of the ancient Hebrew alphabet, the *tav*, was until New Testament times written on Jewish coins as a standing or oblique cross (+ or x). In the Old Testament that letter-sign took on the meaning of a seal that indicates belonging to God, a mark of penitence and protection. It is so used, for instance, in the harsh judgment scene of Ezekiel 9:3-6. When Jesus asked his disciples to take up their cross and follow him, they perhaps understood him to say: Bear and manifest the *tav*. Be wholly devoted to God's purpose and trust God's protection in the final judgment. It is possible that, especially among Jewish Christians, the seal of the *tav* was from early on put on the forehead of those who were baptized. Greek-speaking Christians certainly soon identified this *tav* with the Greek *chi* (χ or +), the first letter of the title "Christ".

For a long time no direct link was made between the sign of the cross and the event at Golgotha. Although from the first generation onwards Christians remembered and confessed the crucifixion of Jesus in worship and teaching, the visible cross sign was strangely absent. As we will see in the next chapter, the cross gained its importance in the churches only from the 4th century, and then not as a symbol of the crucifixion but of the resurrection.

What happened on that first Good Friday was indeed nothing to boast about but rather something to be put into the background. Early Christians in Corinth did so. Instead of the cross they boasted about their deep religious knowledge. The apostle Paul then wrote to them: "We proclaim Christ crucified, a stumbling block to Jews and foolishness to Gentiles, but to those who are called, both Jews and Greeks, Christ the power of God and the wisdom of God" (1 Cor. 1:23-24). In the handwritten postscript of his passionate letter to Christians in Galatia he stated even more radically: "May I never boast of anything except the cross of our Lord Jesus Christ, by which the world has been crucified to me, and I to the world" (Gal. 6:14).

Many are irritated by such radical and often one-sided statements, but in putting the cross in the centre of his gospel message Paul was right. There is no detour around the cross of Jesus. Here we find the most specific and distinctive affirmation of the Way. God certainly has still other ways to bring liberation and healing to the world. Therefore I no longer like to speak about the uniqueness of Christianity if this expression is used to belittle and exclude other living faiths. Yet the centrality given to the cross of Jesus is unique to the Christian faith. Here Paul and many thinkers after him have found the criterion for judging true power and wisdom.

We can only guess what actually happened, probably on a Friday afternoon in spring of the year AD 30, just outside the walls of first-century Jerusalem. After all, this crucifixion did not take place on the main scene of Roman history, but in an outlying province. In Palestine at that time it was only one of hundreds of routine executions. For historians the crucifixion of Jesus remained a hidden event. It was only about a century later that the Roman historian Tacitus mentioned it in a remark about the emperor Nero's persecution of Christians: "Their originator, Christ, had been executed in Tiberius's reign by the governor of Judaea, Pontius Pilatus. But in spite of this temporary setback the deadly superstition had broken out afresh, not only in Judaea, where the mischief had started, but even in Rome. All degraded and shameful practices collect and flourish in that capital" (*Annals* XV, 44).

The first known visual representation of a crucifixion in the Roman empire is like an echo of this derogatory comment. Far from being an artwork it is a crude graffito, scratched on the wall of excavated buildings for the education of imperial pages at the Palatine in Rome (*Fig. 3*). It was probably one of the pupils who drew this caricature: a crucified man with the head of an ass and a second man looking up at him. The inscription reads: "Alexamenos worships his god." In the same building another scratched inscription was discovered which reads like a response to the caricature: "Alexamenos is faithful." Does the graffito refer to Jesus on the cross? Do we have here the remnants of a Christian page being ridiculed? Is the second inscription a responding confession? Although we cannot say for sure, this caricature illustrates well the derision Christians had to face in Roman society, quite apart from the severe persecutions. No wonder they avoided using the cross symbol in public. The earliest

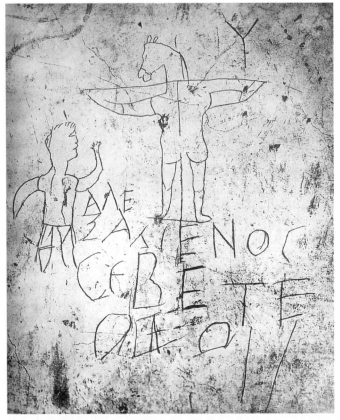

*Fig. 3: Blasphemous drawing of a crucifixion, Rome, early
3rd century*

known *Christian* pictorial representation of Jesus on the
cross dates from the 5th century *(Plate II)*. A meaningful
death confronts a death of desperation. The strong Jesus,
freely giving his life, stands spread out with upright head and
open eyes on the cross, while the greedy Judas hangs dead
and abandoned on a branch that is full of life. Did the artist
interpret Jesus' death in the light of the parable of the mus-
tard seed? What is sown and buried grows into a tree where
"the birds of the air made their nests in the branches".

*Plate II: Earliest known crucifixion scene in Christian art: ivory
tablet, northern Italy, ca. A.D. 420-430*

The event and developing interpretations

What did actually happen at Golgotha? It is not naked facts that speak to us but the gradual unfolding of their significance. The naked fact of Jesus' crucifixion made no sense and was seen only as the miserable end of the story of Jesus. Two of his disciples went home to Emmaus, deeply disappointed: "We hoped, but..." There was something incomprehensible, extraordinary and odd in that historic event. The "king of the Jews" received a cross as his throne and thorns as a crown. The one who had healed many, made miracles and created a new community was now being mocked, helpless and abandoned, abandoned apparently even by God. This strange event called for interpretation, all the more so because his followers soon became convinced that Jesus was alive again.

That Jesus was crucified under Pontius Pilate is a historical fact. What the four New Testament gospels tell about it is at least partly based on eye-witness records and memories. Together with some of Jesus' sayings and healing stories, the passion narratives were the first to be fixed in the oral tradition of the Christian community. They were continuously told and remembered in Christian worship and teaching. No wonder that the crucifixion accounts of all four evangelists follow the same outline: way to the cross, crucifixion, what people who are present do and say, death of Jesus, signs and witnesses of the event. If, within this common structure, the texts are compared in greater detail, divergences immediately appear. The evangelists apparently had access to variously accentuated traditions and then interpreted these differently themselves. This becomes clear if one examines what is reported about the sayings of Jesus on the cross.

The first two evangelists include only one and the same saying, the cry of god-forsakenness, Mark in an Aramaic and Matthew in a Hebrew version. The bystanders misunderstand it as an appeal to Elijah. Luke reports three other sayings and three different ones again are found only in John. Did eye-witnesses hear and understand differently what Jesus may have said in his agony? Or did he really utter all seven sayings, he who during the days before his death had become so strangely silent? Could he in fact have spoken so clearly when he was suffering so much?

Crucifixion was an execution by slow asphyxiation, which implied a desperate struggle for breath. It lasted for many hours, sometimes for days. Having been tortured, the convicts were forced to carry the crossbar to the place of punishment. Their arms were bound or nailed through the wrists to the bar. Then the crossbar was pulled up with the convict and fixed at the top or into an indentation of the already standing vertical pole. The victims did not usually hang on the cross or stand on a footrest, as later Christian art suggests. They were "seated" on a small piece of wood that stuck out in the middle of the pole *(Fig. 4)*. As they became increasingly exhausted they could no longer keep themselves upright and breathing became more and more difficult. According to ancient accounts, the shattering of the victim's legs could shorten the agonies of crucifixion because

Fig. 4

asphyxiation then came quickly. In 1986 many Jews and Christians were struck by the harsh reality of this form of execution when the remains of a crucified young man of Jesus' time were unearthed near Jerusalem. The ossuary contained the skull and the bones, both heels still pierced by a nail. On the basis of an anatomical examination of the skeleton, the archaeologist attempted to reconstruct the position of this crucified man on the cross.

Knowing these hard facts, we must wonder whether Jesus could speak so much and so clearly from the cross. He must have uttered something and died with a cry, as the eye-witnesses reported. What he actually said owes much to later interpretations by the early Christians. By comparing the testimonies in Mark 14, Matthew 27 and Luke 23 we will attempt to discover what these interpretations were (compare and use the parallel texts on *Worksheet B* on pp. 94-95). John's testimony will be discussed in the next chapter.

The disciples were stunned by what happened and the evangelists, too, had no immediate answer. No ready-made "theology of the cross" could expunge the scandal and opaqueness of the event. The accounts of the first three evangelists are not like the deep reflections of Paul about the meaning of the cross, arising from his arguments with opponents and his meditations about true or false faith. Nor does one find (as in John's testimony) any outspoken proof from the scriptures that this happened so a prophetic text could "be fulfilled". Not even Matthew used such a formula here, though he often taught this way in the rest of his gospel. Thus, in the first place, the evangelists transmitted what they had heard from the first generation Christians.

The original witnesses did what every believing Jew would do in such a situation: they turned to the Hebrew scriptures. Could these ancient texts give them any clues towards understanding the still incomprehensible death of Jesus on the cross? The evangelists, too, searched the scriptures for enlightening analogies. The best way to discover the earliest Christian interpretations of the cross is therefore to observe which Old Testament texts are quoted or alluded to in the crucifixion accounts. The results of such an examination are quite astonishing for Christians who still know their creed, catechism and Good Friday liturgies. The key Old Testament texts we would expect to find are absent. In Mark's, Matthew's and Luke's crucifixion accounts there is not a single passage referring to a sacrifice, to substitution, to vicarious suffering, to a death "for our sins". Also missing is the famous song in Isaiah 53 about the suffering servant, which throughout the centuries played such an important role in the interpretation of the death of Jesus.

There are, however, several allusions to Old Testament texts in the evangelists' short crucifixion accounts. No less than four times, verses from Psalm 22 are almost literally quoted: the onlookers' wagging of their heads; the deriding of Jesus; the division of his garments and, above all, the cry: "My God, my God, why have you forsaken me?" Other similar psalms of lament and praise are quoted or alluded to: the friends standing aloof, the poison and vinegar from Psalms 36 and 69 as well as the prayer of confidence from Psalm 31. So Matthew, Mark and Luke tell the crucifixion story in the words of the psalms of lament and praise. This points perhaps to the oldest interpretation of the cross of Jesus: the early Christians had discovered a telling analogy between the fate of Jesus and that described by these psalmists, especially that of the paradigmatic sufferer in Psalm 22. Here they found a key for understanding. Jesus is seen as the Just One who, because he makes God's cause his own, must suffer but will ultimately be vindicated.

A theme with variations

The figure of the righteous/just one played an important role in Jewish spirituality. The Torah, God's command and promise, calls for trust and obedience. It means to care for orphans, widows and landless labourers. It asks the Israelites to love their neighbours as themselves, and also immigrant foreigners. Above all, it is a call to remain faithful to God's covenant, to trust the often hidden God more than tangible idols. Those who walk on this way of the divine command and promise are the righteous, the just ones. During the time before the Babylonian exile in the 6th century BC Israelite believers rather naively assumed that they would be richly rewarded for their obedience in this life and time. Yet the just ones had another life experience. As they sought God's justice for the poor, they had to suffer and became impoverished themselves. The prophets who confronted the powerful with God's will and cause were persecuted. The just ones discovered and accepted the divine "must" of suffering although they could not explain it. They persevered in their trust, walking on God's way until the end, even if it meant martyrdom. In the time of the Maccabees, the period between the Old and the New Testament, the suffering of the martyrs was sometimes understood and interpreted as a suffering for the whole people.

This analogy with the figure of the just one who must suffer opened up for the early Christians a way to understand the crucifixion. Soon other, more specific ways of interpreting the meaning of what happened at Golgotha developed. One of these has become dominant and has marked much of Christian worship and theology. It is the affirmation that Jesus died vicariously for the atonement of the sins: by shedding his blood he became a sacrifice. There is no doubt that this is an old and central New Testament affirmation explaining the scandal of crucifixion. The apostle Paul knew it and developed it further in his letters to the Galatians and the Romans. Variations of this view are found also in the letter to the Hebrews, in 1 Peter and in the book of Revelation. Throughout the centuries the belief in the vicarious death of Jesus for our sins remained a source of consolation. For many it became the very essence of the gospel.

The theme of vicarious suffering will not appear again in these reflections. I do not deny its importance, but it plays no role in the texts being studied: it is almost entirely absent in the whole of Luke's testimony. Moreover, together with many of my contemporaries, I have increasing difficulty with the language of sacrifice, which has too often been misused for oppression. Perhaps I am also too deeply imbued with the strong Old Testament affirmation that human sacrifice is against the will of God. In any case, the understanding of Jesus' death as that of the Just One who must suffer becomes deeply meaningful for life in the present world. It runs like a major theme through the first three gospels and the Acts. In their crucifixion accounts, each of the evangelists develops his own variation.

Mark's whole gospel leads up to the passion. It is the long way of the hidden messianic king to the cross. The Christians for whom Mark wrote probably knew Jesus mainly or exclusively as a healer and miracle worker, full of power. This is not wrong and in the first part of the gospel Mark told many healing stories. But such one-sided belief had to be corrected, and in the latter half of the gospel accounts of healings become sparse. During the final stretch Jesus is portrayed as weak. He breaks down while carrying the cross bar. In the decisive hour when people want to see a miracle and when they challenge him to come down from the cross and save himself, Jesus disappoints their expectations. His disciples have misunderstood his way of being the messianic king and have already fled. At the end there is only the cry to God who also seems to have abandoned him. Then a miracle happens: not only the signs but especially the affirmation of the Roman officer: "Truly, this man was God's son." If the centurion indeed said this, he probably meant no more than, "Here was an extraordinary, godly man." For Mark and the early Christians this statement became the confession that Jesus, the suffering and crucified Just One, is the messianic king. In the agony of the cross the decisive struggle with evil takes place. Mark's crucifixion account can thus best be read as a call and encouragement to faith, to follow Jesus and to bear his cross.

Matthew also recounts the events at Golgotha with the language of the psalms of lament and praise. In Mark's testimony Jesus remains until the end the hidden messianic king. Matthew portrays him more as the authoritative teacher, full of God's wisdom. Jesus receives this authority by doing God's will and by trusting God until the last. Only in Matthew's account is the trust of the suffering righteous one from Psalm 22 actually referred to by the Jewish authorities: "He trusts in God; let God deliver him now, if he wants to." There is also a striking parallel with the temptation story where the devil says to Jesus on the pinnacle of the temple, "If you are the Son of God, throw yourself down." Now the Jewish authorities and those who pass by challenge the crucified: "If you are the Son of God, come down from the cross." Crucifixion is seen here as a last temptation. In Matthew's account of the prayer-struggle in Gethsemane Jesus finally can say to God, "Your will be done." Now, on the cross, Jesus proves himself to be the Just One and the Son of God precisely because he withstands the temptation and perseveres in trust, even within his god-forsakenness. The accompanying signs, which Matthew has expanded, show that God is present and that, paradoxically, crucifixion becomes an enthronement. Not only the Roman officer but also "those with him" acknowledge that "truly this man was God's son". People outside the circle of Jesus' followers, non-Jews, are already beginning to confess the messianic king. For the Christians of "little belief", as Matthew portrays the disciples, crucifixion thus becomes both a message of hope and a call to perseverance.

Luke most strongly emphasizes the understanding of Jesus' death as that of God's suffering Just One. According to his account, the Roman officer "praised God and said, 'Certainly, this man was innocent/just.'" Probably he only affirmed that Jesus was an innocent victim, repeating what one of the criminals crucified with him had already stated. For Luke and the early church this Roman officer becomes the first non-Jewish convert. In the passion stories of all four gospels a short quotation from Isaiah 53 occurs only once: in Luke 22:37 Jesus says that in him is fulfilled the word that the suffering servant "was counted among the lawless". This does not refer to vicarious sacrifice but to God's servant as the innocently suffering Just One (a later copyist transferred this quotation into Mark's crucifixion account – Mark 15:28 – a verse that is rightly omitted in modern translations, since it is missing in the old manuscripts.) Just like God's servant in the book of Isaiah, Jesus remains confident in the midst of suffering. Instead of the cry of god-forsakenness Jesus prays confidently, "Father, into your hands I commend my spirit." One who has such an intimate relation with God brings both the judging and the forgiving God near to those who meet him. In Luke's account, on the way to the cross Jesus warns the crowd and the lamenting women that judgment is near. Implicitly that judgment then comes on those who mock him on the cross and Luke places the rending of the temple curtain before Jesus' death. The emphasis, though, is more strongly on forgiveness. In a saying (which is not well attested in old manuscripts) the crucified intercedes for his torturers: "Father, forgive them; for they do not know what they are doing." He even makes a promise to the criminal on his right-hand side: "Today you will be with me in Paradise." "Today" is a term Luke favours. Where Jesus comes with the power of the Spirit, things begin to happen: healing, blessedness and conversion. It is significant that, in Luke's account, Simon of Cyrene is seized to carry the cross "behind Jesus". In a literal sense he is the first follower and cross-bearer. Also, the crowd present at the crucifixion shows signs of repentance: they "returned home, beating their breasts". So Luke's testimony can best be seen as a call to repentance and discipleship, an encouragement to receive forgiveness.

The signs

Mark reports: "It was nine o'clock in the morning when they crucified him.... When it was noon, darkness came over the whole land until three in the afternoon. At three o'clock Jesus cried out with a loud voice, 'Eloi. Eloi'... Then Jesus gave a loud cry and breathed his last. And the curtain of the temple was torn in two, from top to bottom." The eye-witnesses present must have seen some astonishing phenomena, but what precisely took place we can no longer know.

Mark insists that crucifixion happened step by step, in Jewish reckoning of time, from the third to the ninth and the twelfth hour. It is like a drama with three acts leading up to a final climax. In Jewish apocalyptic visions such an inescapable sequence of time spans leads up to a cosmic crisis, to judgment and a new creation. Matthew and Luke do not record this full scheme of hours, but they also mention the sudden frightening darkness that Luke explains as an eclipse of the sun. Darkness can be variously interpreted. In prophetic-apocalyptic literature it is often associated with judgment. Luke actually refers to such a judgment passage (Hos. 10:8) in what Jesus said to the woman on the way to Golgotha. No Old Testament text is clearly recalled in the verses about what happened from the sixth to the ninth hour. These verses may possibly point to the coming judgment which is now already affecting those who have condemned and mocked, who are now killing the innocent, who are, at that very moment, being judged. The phenomenon of darkness can also be explained as recalling the dark cosmic sea in the first verses of the Bible. "Darkness covered the face of the deep" before God spoke the creative words, "Let there be light". Although it is not explicitly stated, darkness indeed ended and light returned at the very moment when Jesus died. Crucifixion, then, means not only a judgment but also a new creation.

The rending of the temple curtain has received as many different interpretations as the metaphor of darkness. It concerns the temple that Herod the Great had begun to rebuild, magnificently enlarging the second temple built in the Persian period. Nothing but part of the esplanade of the temple hill remains. Are the evangelists referring to the veil which, within the temple, separated the holy sanctuary from the dark and empty most holy inner shrine that only the high priest could enter? Do they mean the curtain separating the temple building from the surrounding temple courts? Or does the curtain symbolize the whole temple complex and temple worship? The metaphor of the torn veil might therefore indicate the crisis besetting Jewish temple worship. It can be seen as the abolition of the separation between the priests and the people or between the Jews and the Gentiles. It can even be understood to mean that, through the cross of Jesus, a gate between heaven and earth has been opened.

Matthew reports still other extraordinary signs. "The earth shook, and the rocks were split. The tombs also were opened, and many bodies of the saints who had fallen asleep were raised." A formidable reversal takes place. As the obedient Just One dies the buried saints rise to life. The term "saint", applied to people, occurs only here in Matthew's gospel. The evangelist and the early Christians probably thought of faithful Israelites, the just and poor ones of God, persecuted prophets and martyrs. Has the end come? People had already wondered whether Jesus was calling for Elijah, initiating the messianic age. Earthquakes are signs of the final cataclysm. There are also Old Testament passages where, as at Mount Sinai, the shaking earth points to a theophany, to the manifestation of the presence of God. Those who mocked and judged their king are judged themselves and the darkness is for them. Those who thought that God was absent and had abandoned Jesus now experience the awe-full presence of God. What happened on the outskirts of the Roman empire in an almost hidden way is confessed as the crucial point of world history.

* * *

The above possible interpretations of the signs that accompanied Jesus' death tend to outshine what really happened at Golgotha, transforming it into a success story and a theology of glory. It is therefore important not to forget the early Christian understanding of the crucifixion: the death of the Just One ready to give his life. This interpretation of the cross has in modern times become deeply meaningful for those involved in costly struggles for freedom and justice, for peace and responsible stewardship of the creation's resources. They see a long road of labour ahead of them. Often they live with broken hopes and expectations and feel like burnt-out cases. In their struggles they have at times been enmeshed in evil. Therefore they need the healing of forgiveness and an upholding network of those who continue to walk behind the suffering Just One. They know that what is needed is a multitude of *given* lives.

The parable hidden in the Coptic tapestry speaks strongly for their situation. It teaches that the cross is not the banner of a triumphant victory it became in the Constantinian period. Nor is it primarily the symbol of suffering and death it became in the middle ages. It is the symbol of given life, making human community possible. Each fabric shows us this truth. True, Jesus' crucifixion led to the hour when the fabric of the temple curtain was torn apart. In my attempt to conceive a tapestry for Good Friday it was this sign that spoke strongly to me and I tried to weave a torn curtain: what a paradox! Much tearing apart and opening up will still be needed in our individual and corporate life as Christians and world citizens. Crucifixion, though, does not point only to such a judging, painful and ultimately healing rending-apart. It also leads to a new wholeness made possible by the given life of the Just One and of his followers. In a tapestry only a multitude of invisible crosses can create flexibility and consistency. So the fabric of the human community is woven together only through a multitude of given lives. What a given life means can be learned by following the way of the Just One to the cross.

3. The Living

"Why do you look for the living among the dead? He is not here, but has risen!" So two men in dazzling clothes spoke to the women who came to the tomb early on Easter morning. What did they see and hear? The resurrection of Jesus remains a great mystery, an elusive event. The crucifixion could have been photographed and filmed, an event of history within history. With the resurrection, a reality from beyond our time broke into human history. It was neither the resuscitation of a dead man's body nor a mere projection of faith told as a historic event. Something *did* happen. Even the Roman historian Tacitus had to acknowledge that what he called "a deadly superstition" was checked for a moment with Jesus' death but broke out afresh and even came to Rome. Having met the risen Lord, the few fearful first disciples soon become audacious witnesses. "Christ has risen!" they proclaimed. What did they feel when they made this affirmation? And how have Christians since then envisaged this mysterious event that has become so central in their worship and message? The development of Christian art is revealing in this respect.

Attempting to see the invisible

Christian art had a slow beginning. Strong arguments could be used against its development. Like the Jews, the early Christians obeyed the biblical prohibition against making images of God. Many idols were worshipped in the Greek and Roman world. Moreover, in the Bible the word is given priority over the image. The gospels were written in the latter half of the first century AD, but the earliest remnants of Christian art date only from the 3rd century, when wall paintings in the catacombs of Rome show scenes from the Old Testament and Jesus is depicted as the good shepherd. The Christ monogram, the Chi-Rho sign (☧) formed by the first two Greek letters of the title Christ, begins to appear. Alongside it are other symbols like the anchor, the fish, a ship, a bird and loaves of bread (*Plate III*), visual prayers for salvation and confessions of hope in the burial place. More figurative paintings depict baptism, the coming

Plate III: Wall paintings in early Christian catacombs, Rome, 3rd and 4th century

of the magi, healing miracles, holy meals and figures of praying faithful. There still is no direct visual evocation or portrayal of either Jesus' crucifixion or his resurrection.

It is only in the middle of the 4th century that a first clear visual pointer to the resurrection appears. From then on scenes of the passion story are represented on Christian sarcophagi (stone coffins adorned with sculptured reliefs). The centre-piece of one such sarcophagus, in Rome, shows the Christ monogram in a triumphal wreath of laurels (*Plate IV*). In the upper corners stand the sun and the moon. On the crossbar two birds feed from the laurel crown. Under the cross sit two Roman soldiers, one looking up and the other, with closed eyes, leaning on his shield. On either side of this symbolic centre-piece, other reliefs depict four scenes realistically: Simon of Cyrene carrying the cross, a Roman soldier crowning Jesus, Jesus being led before Pilate and, finally, the hesitant Pilate washing his hands. Here the harsh passion story of the gospels becomes a victory story as former events are reinterpreted in the light of Jesus' resurrection. The crown is no longer made of thorns but of laurels, like those given to victorious emperors. Jesus holds in his hands the scroll of the gospel. Led before Pilate, he stands majestically with a raised hand, speaking. The small figure of Pilate turns his face away as if he is ashamed and afraid.

This first visual evocation of the resurrection is intimately linked to a victorious battle of Constantine the Great in 312. Already aware of the event's legendary potential, Constantine told his biographer, Eusebius of Caesarea, what had happened just before that battle. "He said that about noon, when the day was already beginning to decline, he saw with his own eyes the trophy of the cross of light in the heavens, above the sun, and bearing the inscription, 'Conquer by this!'" Amazed, Constantine "doubted within himself what the import of this apparition could be. And while he continued to ponder and reason on its meaning, night suddenly came on. Then in his sleep the Christ of God appeared to him with the same sign which he had seen in the heavens, and commanded him to make a likeness of that sign which he had seen." Euse-

*Plate IV: Passion
sarcophagus, Rome,
ca. 340*

bius goes on to describe how Constantine immediately had a new army standard made. It took the form of a cross on the top of which "was fixed a wreath of gold and precious stones; and within this, the symbol of the Saviour's name, two letters indicating the name of Christ" (*The Life of Constantine*, I.28-31). The cross with the Christ monogram became the emblem of the army of the first Christian emperor, and from this emblem stems the first resurrection art. A year later an edict of tolerance brought the end of severe persecutions of Christians in the Roman empire.

This military and imperial origin of the invincible cross, the symbol for Jesus' rising from the dead, is a matter of embarrassment for many Christians today. If we read the church history of Eusebius, full of recurring martyr stories during the cruel persecutions, we can understand that Christians of the 4th century saw a strong analogy between Constantine's victory and that of the risen Jesus. The invincible cross in Christian art was soon adorned with precious stones and lifted up into the heavens. Unfortunately this was done not only to the glory of God; it also served to glorify a triumphal empire and church. Before long this led to the persecution of Jews and others who did not accept Christianity.

An eagle, Jupiter's bird, appears in the passion/victory sarcophagus described earlier, bringing down the imperial wreath and covering with his wings the triumphant cross. Perhaps the artist already knew the stories of a popular Christian book, the *Physiologus*, which was widely circulated and translated. It tells about animals, some stones and plants, interpreting their symbolism for the Christian faith. The eagle appears there as a mighty symbol for the resurrection and ascension of Jesus because that bird was said to fly highest and to be able to look into the sun. The *Physiologus* mentions three other animals who prefigure the resurrection through their behaviour: the lion, the pelican and the phoenix. Together with the eagle they are later often depicted in Easter art. In sleep, the lion always keeps his eyes open and his breath brings still-born cubs back to life. The young ones of the pelican live again three days after their death, revived by the blood of their mother who tears open her breast. The mythological phoenix dies in the fire of the altar to be reborn out of the flames. Besides such analogies from the animal world some Old Testament figures function as a visual prefiguration of the resurrection: Jonah, rescued from the whale, and Samson with his mighty deeds. Until the early middle ages, however, Jesus' actual rising from the tomb was only proclaimed, liturgically celebrated and pointed to symbolically; in Western art it was never visually portrayed.

Eastern and Western resurrection art

Among the Orthodox churches Easter is not only one among the feasts but *the* feast. Nevertheless, the rich iconography of the Eastern churches never represents the actual event of the resurrection. There are, though, icons of the rising of Lazarus, which can function as an analogy. During Easter celebrations two other icons become prominent. One recalls the visit of the women at the already empty tomb, told in all four gospels (this scene probably appears on a much damaged 3rd-century wall painting in a Christian home in Doura-Europos in Syria). The second Easter icon portrays Jesus' descent into hell. This affirmation of faith was never made in the New Testament gospels and is only hinted at in 1 Peter. A dramatic description of the descent to hell is included in the late apocryphal gospel of Nicodemus. Visual representations of the descent appeared late, only from AD 700 onwards, and they show Jesus, a day before his resurrection, already defeating the powers of death.

In the Western church, popular spirituality asked for more than symbols and analogies. Believers wanted to see the invisible. Contrary to the testimony of the evangelists, who never describe how Jesus rose from the dead, medieval book illuminators began to portray that event. From the 11th century onwards manuscripts of the psalms show Jesus stepping out of his tomb. At first rare, this illumination became increasingly popular. The risen Lord sometimes steps on the heads of the guarding soldiers or stands on the still closed but now empty tomb. In the late middle ages this resurrection

*Plate V: Embroidered Easter tapestry of Lüne convent,
northern Germany, 1503-1515*

scene is literally put into the centre of the universe, for instance in a large embroidered Easter tapestry from northern Germany (*Plate V*). At the centre of two concentric circles Jesus rises from his tomb. The inner circle takes the form of a seven-cornered star and the inscription proclaims the risen Lord as the morning star and the Alpha and Omega, the beginning and the end. In between the corners of the star stand seven angels playing musical instruments, symbolizing the seven days. Around the outer circle are 12 bells (the 12 hours) and 12 moons (the 12 months). In the four corners of the tapestry appear the eagle, the phoenix, the pelican and the lion. On top of the whole composition stands the sun and at the bottom the tree of life. The event of Jesus' resurrection is thus envisioned as the focus of all times and of the whole cosmos. From around 1500, in the numerous resurrection depictions, the rising Jesus appears already lifted up, soaring in the air as a majestic figure. This is the case, for instance, in the famous resurrection woodcut by Albrecht Dürer or in the paintings of Matthias Grünewald and El Greco.

During more recent centuries there have been fewer visual representations of the resurrection, but I am not sorry about this scarcity. However imaginative and artful such Western visions of the mystery of Easter may be, they make me uneasy. Do they not make the invisible too clearly visible? In fact these representations of the rising Lord owe more to apocryphal writings than to the New Testament. In the 2nd century, the apocryphal gospel of Peter dramatically described the resurrection, writing that the soldiers guarding the tomb heard "a loud voice in heaven, and they saw the heavens opened and two men come down from there in great brightness and draw nigh to the sepulchre. That stone which had been laid against the entrance to the sepulchre started of itself to roll and gave way the side, and the sepulchre was opened, and both the young men entered in." The guards woke the centurion and the elders who were helping to watch the tomb. Then "they saw again three men come out of the sepulchre, and two of them sustained the other, and a cross following them, and the heads of the two reaching to heaven, but that of him who was led of them by the hand overpassing the heavens. And they heard a voice out of the heavens crying, 'Thou hast preached to them that sleep', and from the cross there was heard the answer, 'Yea'" (gospel of Peter, 9:36-10:42). This could well function as the scenario for a dramatic religious motion picture, but it is not the New Testament message about the resurrection.

The transparent cross

For grasping what the evangelists testify about Easter morning it is helpful to start with the gospel of John and, paradoxically, with his passion story (John 18-19). Some interpreters assume that it must have been a great problem for John to incorporate the passion and crucifixion into his testimony about Jesus. Does he not show us Jesus even from before creation and throughout his journey as the Son of God, as the light, the life and the truth? Does he not present the one sent by God as one who comes from the heavenly world and returns to the glory of that world beyond? John's gospel contains no announcements of suffering like those reported by Mark, Matthew and Luke. Instead Jesus declares that he will be lifted up, exalted and that he will enter into the glory of God.

There are elements in the passion story of the fourth gospel that can lead to the conclusion that John saw Jesus' cross simply as a royal step upwards on the ladder to glory. Several inversions are reported, almost tragicomic scenes. When Jesus is arrested, it is not he and his disciples who are afraid but the detachment of soldiers and the police of the Jewish authorities: "They stepped back and fell to the ground." In the trial scene two different kinds of kingship confront each other and it is Pilate who declares Jesus to be the king of the Jews. According to a possible translation of the original text, it is not Pilate but Jesus who sits on the judge's bench. In their argument with the Roman procurator the Jewish authorities deny their own God and confess the Roman emperor to be their king.

In stressing Jesus' authority, John's account of the crucifixion differs significantly from the reports of the other evangelists. Jesus does not break down on the way to Golgotha and he himself carries the crossbar. Despite Jewish protests, the tablet on the cross publicly declares him, in three languages, to be the king. A sudden darkness does not occur nor is the rending of the temple curtain mentioned. Neither the people who pass by nor those who are crucified with him revile Jesus. His own family and friends do not totally abandon him. From the cross Jesus creates community by addressing his mother and the beloved disciple who stand nearby, committing them to one another's care. So Jesus is not described as one who passively suffers until the end but as the one who takes initiatives and fulfils scriptural prophecies. Thus the soldiers have to cast lots for his seamless tunic as the quoted psalm had prophesied. Jesus' saying, "I am thirsty", is reported as a fulfilment of a psalm. In the end there is neither a cry of abandonment nor a prayer, but the confident affirmation: "It is finished/accomplished." What has come to its end and is now accomplished is the will and work of God who sent him to do this. Then Jesus "bowed his head and gave up his spirit".

These examples must not, however, mislead us into forgetting that John's testimony also shows Jesus enduring humiliation and death. His crown is of thorns, not of laurels. There is torture and mockery before Golgotha. No reversal occurs at the crucifixion itself. In fact, John places a strong and realistic emphasis on the actual death. There is no need to break Jesus' legs so that he will die quickly before the sabbath: he is already dead, and a soldier pierces his side. These two incidents, not recorded by the other evangelists, are again told as a fulfilment of scriptural passages. Obviously there are deep symbolic meanings in these events, but their first significance is that Jesus physically died.

Two apparently contradictory trends appear: on the one side incarnation leading to death, on the other elevation leading to glory. John shows us Jesus taking part fully in a very earthly, material existence in this world and at the same time remaining in a continuous union with the splendour of God's world. How can such a double emphasis be brought together? Probably the best key to understanding John's way of witnessing to Jesus is to interpret his whole gospel as one great transfiguration story.

This most Johannine scene in Jesus' life, his transfiguration on the mountain reported by all other evangelists, is not included in the fourth gospel, and as we read through the whole of John's testimony we discover the reason for this amazing "omission". The glory of the divine world shines through the often dark human and physical realities of all Jesus' time on earth and not only on the mount of transfiguration. John writes as icon painters paint. They do not use oils, which cover everything, but paint with slightly transparent colours made of yolk and pigments. The gleaming white priming of chalk and alabaster and thin gold sheets placed on parts of the priming shine through the subsequent layers of colours. Light comes from within and the icons make transfigured reality visible. This reality is seen from God's point of view, signified by the inverted perspective used in icon painting. John's gospel resembles such an icon: the total life and ministry of Jesus, as well as what happened at the cross, are seen in the light of transfiguration and resurrection.

For John, crucifixion is not simply a step towards elevation. Matthew links crucifixion and resurrection by testifying that Jesus' death triggers the rising of the "saints", but John goes one step further: he tells the crucifixion as an integral part of the resurrection. By the cross and still on the cross Jesus accomplishes the work and will of his heavenly Father. His hour has come. "Having loved his own who were in the world, he loved them to the end." He gives his life for the salvation of the world (13:1, 3:16). The divine "must" of passion is revealed as the "must" of divine love. The only passage where the fourth evangelist insists on his authority as an eye-witness is when he reports the piercing of the side of the already dead Jesus: he does so "that you also may believe". Belief comes from recognizing the victory of resurrection in seeing Jesus crucified. According to the gospels, this is the only way to see the invisible. How could resurrection be visually portrayed except through a cross, yet a cross that becomes a window for the life and light of the divine world? In this way glimpses of divine reality are given to us right within and through human reality.

The attempt to express this elusive and mysterious character of resurrection in a tapestry went far beyond my dilettante weaving skills. A 20th-century German sculptor, Friedrich Press, has captured much of what I think the evangelists testify about rising of Jesus. His relief "Resurrection" (*Plate VI*) , carved in a large plank of pine, visualizes it with evocative simplicity.

Luke's narrative of the resurrection

After the testimony of John we turn to the narratives of Luke, where the resurrection is more clearly separated from the crucifixion, and from Jesus' ascension, which occurs 40 days later. Neither Matthew nor John recount such an ascension story and it is referred to briefly only in a later addition to Mark's gospel. The double account of the ascension becomes, in fact, the turning point in Luke's narratives. After Jesus' earthly ministry attention now centres on what the risen and ascended Lord continues to do through the power of the Holy Spirit. According to John, the risen Lord imparted the Spirit on the eve of Easter; Luke places it 50 days after the resurrection during the Jewish feast of Pentecost. Based on Luke's testimony, the ancient church then gradually developed the cycle of Christian feasts.

Reading the resurrection accounts in the New Testament one wonders whether on Easter morning we should say "Happy Easter" to one another. The first witnesses, in any case, did not immediately dance with joy. According to Mark, the women fled from the empty tomb, "for terror and amazement had seized them; and they said nothing to anyone, for they were afraid". Strange, to end a gospel of good news in such a way. Matthew reports that the women "left the tomb quickly with fear and great joy, and ran to tell the disciples". In John's gospel there is first weeping and then the puzzled search for Jesus' body. Later the beloved disciple

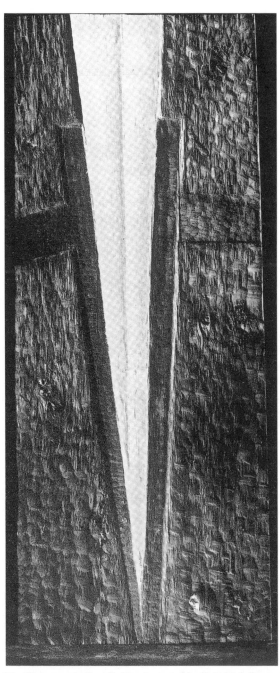

Plate VI: "Resurrection", relief in pinewood by Friedrich Press, 1983

"saw and believed", but he saw only the empty tomb. It was Mary Magdalene whom the risen Lord met and she became the first witness of the resurrection.

In Luke's account (24:1-12) very little happens and certainly nothing of the dramatic events recorded in the apocryphal writings mentioned earlier. Even compared with the canonical gospels, Luke, the gifted story-teller, gives a very sober account. Only Mark reports that the women coming to anoint the body wondered who would roll away the stone from the tomb. As in his crucifixion account, Matthew again describes an earthquake. He also writes about the terrified guards and the angel of the Lord who rolls back the stone from the already empty grave. John describes Peter and the beloved disciple running to the tomb and then the first appearance of the risen Lord. There is none of this action in Luke's narrative, only the open, empty tomb. The perplexed women receive no message to deliver from the two men in dazzling clothes. They are simply helped to remember what Jesus had told them in Galilee, that "the Son of Man must be handed over to sinners, and be crucified, and on the third day rise again". Here the expression "Son of Man" clearly refers to the man Jesus, especially as suffering prophet, replacing the "I". Despite the empty tomb and the words of the messengers the women gain no new insight and faith. True, now they remember Jesus' announcements. They also tell the disciples what they have seen and heard, but their report is considered only "an idle tale", nonsense. For Peter, too, who immediately runs to the burial place, the empty tomb does not lead to faith.

A strange encounter

There is both tragedy and comedy in what Luke relates about the first appearance of the risen Jesus (24:13-35). Two disciples walk home to Emmaus, a village whose site remains uncertain. One of them is Cleopas, whom later sources identify as an uncle or cousin of Jesus. It may well be that the Emmaus story, not transmitted by other evangelists, belonged to a tradition of the Jesus family. The two who go home are surly and deeply disappointed. Even when the risen Jesus joins their journey they do not recognize him. Shocked by his ignorance, they tell him the Jesus story from their own point of view. It is the story of a man, "a prophet mighty in deed and word before God and all the people", who had been handed over to be crucified. They had hoped "that he was the one who would redeem/liberate Israel". This hope for redemption or liberation of the people of Israel is mentioned in the birth narratives of Luke's gospel, clearly in connection with the promised and expected coming kingdom of David. What the two on the way to Emmaus explain to the astonishingly uninformed stranger is what Jesus' disciples believed up to Easter eve: not a completely wrong but only a partial understanding of Jesus' ministry. Still puzzled, they add what they have heard about the empty tomb and about the women's report, but for them the crucifixion remains the end of the story. No weight is given to women talking about their "vision of angels".

At this point even the risen Jesus loses his patience: "Oh, how foolish you are, and how slow of heart to believe all that the prophets have declared! Was it not necessary that the Christ/Messiah should suffer these things and then enter into his glory?" This is the first passage in Luke's gospel where Jesus speaks about himself as the Christ, the Messiah. His life, death and resurrection have given that title new meaning, different from the expected Davidic messianic king. Jesus then continues to do what he did during his earthly ministry: he teaches the slow believers about the purpose of God and he does so by interpreting the Jewish scriptures, "beginning with Moses and all the prophets". (During his later appearance among his disciples in Jerusalem the psalms are added to Moses and the prophets.)

No specific Old Testament passage is mentioned here. Are we to understand that Jesus is the "prophet like Moses" (Deut. 18:15-18) who would come? Is he the prophet Elijah who would return at the end of times (Mal. 4:5-6) and who was taken up into heaven (a Jewish tradition also tells of such an ascent of Moses)? Is he the suffering Servant of the book of Isaiah? Or is he the suffering Just One who must suffer but will be vindicated, as Psalm 22, interpreted as a prophecy, announces? It would certainly be wrong to restrict Jesus' interpretation of the scriptures to just one passage or a few excerpts. What Luke emphasizes is, rather, a pattern of prophetic and servant destiny. Jesus is linked with messengers of God before him and his life is seen as a pattern for those who follow him. Later Stephen, the martyr, will interpret the scriptures in a similar way (Acts 7).

Now things begin to happen. The disciples do not yet recognize Jesus, but later they say to one another: "Were not our hearts burning within us while he was talking to us on the road, while he was opening the scriptures to us?" During his appearances among the disciples at Emmaus and at Jerusalem Jesus "opens up" three times: here he opens the Hebrew scriptures, at the meal he opens their eyes and later he opens their minds to understanding. Jesus thus remains not only the teacher but also the healer. He heals the disciples' blindness and slowness.

How slow, indeed, is the disciples' growth of understanding. The empty tomb did not lead to faith, nor the recalling of what Jesus himself had announced about his destiny. The Hebrew scriptures had not helped them to recognize how Jesus would become the prophet and a new type of Messiah. Not even the presence of the risen Lord and his interpreting of the scriptures was enough to lead the disciples to faith. Their burning hearts lead nevertheless to their wish to remain in his presence. Only at the meal do they finally recognize him.

The gestures of Jesus

"When he was at the table with them, he took bread, blessed and broke it, and gave it to them. Then their eyes were opened, and they recognized him." This is the eighth time that Luke describes Jesus taking a meal with others and teaching them. This time there is no further oral instruction. Jesus teaches with gestures. Two similar incidents had already happened. At the feeding of the multitude (9:10-17) he took five loaves of bread and two fish. "He looked up to heaven, and blessed and broke them, and gave them to the disciples to set before the crowd." At the Last Supper

(22:14-20) "he took a loaf of bread, and when he had given thanks, he broke it and gave it to them". To "bless" and to "give thanks" mean essentially the same: both acknowledge the majesty and goodness of God. The table fellowship at Emmaus was probably an ordinary meal, yet it was the familiar gesture of breaking the bread that finally triggered the disciples' recognition. When they run back to Jerusalem, the two disciples tell "how he had been made known to them in the breaking of the bread".

At several crucial moments Jesus taught more by significant gestures than by words, for instance when healing, when receiving children, when entering Jerusalem, when driving merchants out of the temple court and especially during the Last Supper with the disciples before his crucifixion. Time was running out and the disciples still did not understand. On that solemn occasion Jesus therefore once again summed up his whole ministry in a series of gestures: taking and receiving from God's creation and human labour bread and wine, blessing and giving thanks for them, breaking the bread and pouring out the wine, giving and sharing them. He added only a few words. In Hebrew thinking, "body" refers to the whole bodily existence: "This is my body" means, in the first place, "This is me." Blood refers to life: "This is my blood" means, in the first place, "This is my life." Whatever deep meanings these sayings of Jesus received in the course of later interpretations, this primary meaning must not be forgotten. Jesus then added, "Do this in remembrance of me." With these words he was not only asking his disciples to go on celebrating the Lord's supper or to think of him from time to time: he was using the term remembrance in the strong Hebrew sense of becoming a participant in what is remembered. Receiving Jesus' gift of himself, the disciples are called to enter into the pattern of his life, summed up visually through gesture.

* * *

"And he vanished from their sight." What an anti-climax! Now that the disciples had finally recognized him and that he was bodily present with them, he vanished. He was entering into God's glory and could not be fixed for human sight. Until today the risen Jesus remains an elusive presence. Neither Christian art nor the study of biblical texts solves for us the mystery of resurrection. Only by recognizing the living one in the dead one on the cross can our human realities sometimes become transparent for the light and glory of divine reality. More than this is not given to us. We have the Hebrew scriptures to reinterpret in the light of Jesus' ministry and destiny. We have the apostles' and the evangelists' testimonies about what they remembered and understood about his words, deeds and death. We received the promise that God's Spirit will empower us. We also have the meal, summing up the pattern of Jesus' life. None of this is proof of resurrection, but it gives us enough reason to continue walking according to the Way. In faith we can say to one another, "Christ has risen!", and respond, "He has truly risen!"

When I get swept away by the self-seeking patterns of life I sometimes like to make for myself the gestures of the Lord's supper: receiving and taking, blessing and giving thanks, breaking and pouring out, giving and sharing. With my body I try to enter into the pattern of his life.

Readers may want to do the same at the close of these Easter reflections.

4. The Wind of the Spirit

It happened between two islands in a widely scattered Indonesian archipelago. With a local pastor I was visiting isolated Christian congregations to direct training courses. We sat in a narrow *prahu*, a dugout tree trunk with outriggers and a makeshift sail. There was no wind. The two villagers who were acting as guides suddenly began to row as if they were in a race. I did not see the danger, but later they told me that, in this region, dangerous sea currents could carry small boats far out into the sea where they were often lost. They rowed with frenzy, but our *prahu* continued to drift away from our island destination. Then a wind came up. With the sail catching it and further hard rowing we escaped the current. No pious words were spoken and nothing really extraordinary happened. Nevertheless, whenever the spirit of this age overwhelms me, I remember that long-ago incident: for me it has become a parable for Pentecost.

When I am reflecting on the Holy Spirit I intentionally start with a personal experience and one that is out in the midst of God's creation. Many Christians tend to limit the Spirit only to what happens in the life of the churches or to "spiritualize" too quickly what we celebrate at Pentecost. As we will see, there is a strong link in the New Testament between Jesus and God's Spirit and an intimate connection between Pentecost and Christian mission. But the creative and life-giving energy of the Spirit was at work long before New Testament times, since the very beginning of this world. The Spirit touches people and communities in the middle of daily life. Its energy is sometimes a hardly perceptible breeze and sometimes an extraordinary, unexpected blast.

A page of visual theology

In the late middle ages Benedictine monks made a small manual for biblical teaching, the *Biblia Pauperum*, which originally contained 34 visual lessons. In each of these a central drawing pointed to a key event from the gospels, fixed for the eyes and interpreted by the pronouncements of four prophets who surrounded the illustration. Also, two Old Testament stories were recalled as prefigurations of the lesson's

New Testament event. Whenever monks and parish priests who had no access to a full manuscript of the Bible leafed through this small booklet, they discovered connections between the two testaments and were taught a whole biblical theology. Many today would not agree with the book's content, which is that of the medieval Western church, but the way of teaching remains exemplary. Artist and biblical interpreters together might well create a *Biblia Pauperum* for the biblical illiterates of our own time and thus help Christians to see and understand the Bible as a whole.

The page on Pentecost reproduced in *Plate VII* comes from a richly coloured early 15th-century German manuscript. The central scene, with the gift of the Spirit, is prefigured by Moses receiving the Torah on Mount Sinai and Elijah receiving the fire for the sacrifice on Mount Carmel. The associated prophetic oracles break open the frame of the history of the Israelites. They point to the beginning and the end of the universe.

The first two prophecies recall a basic biblical affirmation of faith: the whole universe was created through the word, the wisdom and the Spirit of God. David, who in the middle ages was seen as the prophet of the psalms, quotes Psalm 33:6. Around his portrait is written the beginning of the announcement: "By the word of the Lord the heavens were made, and all their host by the breath of his mouth." Many other similar passages could have been quoted, especially from Psalm 104. The first two chapters of the Bible also come to mind. The wind of God's Spirit sweeps over the dark chaos as creation is ordered and becomes "very good". The breath of God gives life to human beings. The second prophet is Jesus Sirach, the author of a deutero-canonical wisdom book. He actually quotes not from his own writing but from the Wisdom of Solomon, a similar book: "The Spirit of the Lord has filled the world" (Wis. 1:7). Already in Proverbs 8-9, and even more strongly in the just mentioned deutero-canonical books, God's Spirit is related to the often personified Wisdom, associated both with God's creative work and with the beauty of creation.

Plate VII: Pentecost page of the Biblia Pauperum, *Heidelberg manuscript, early 15th century*

The two other prophetic oracles deal with the role of the Spirit in the divine renewing and re-creating work. According to Ezekiel, God promised to the Israelites that, in spite of their defilement, "I will put my spirit within you" (36:27). This stands in the context of the promised final peace and blessing when both the land and the people will be cleansed and there will be abundant life as in the garden of Eden. A similar promise is uttered by the prophet Joel, a passage that Peter actually quoted in his proclamation at Pentecost: "I will pour out my spirit on all flesh; your sons and your daughters shall prophesy, your old men shall dream dreams, and your young men shall see visions. Even on the male and female slaves, in those days, I will pour out my spirit" (Joel 2:28ff.).

The first Old Testament story recalled on this page of the *Biblia Pauperum* often appears in medieval art as a prefiguration of Pentecost: Moses, Aaron and the elders went up to Mount Sinai where "they saw the God of Israel" and where Moses received the Torah (Ex. 24:9ff.). In the time of Jesus the original agricultural Jewish festival of Pentecost was related to the renewal of God's covenants with Noah, Abraham and Moses. Later rabbinical teaching also linked it with the giving of the Torah. In the drawing of the Heidelberg manuscript God appears without the fire and earthquake described in Exodus. The accent lies on the renewed meeting with God. No tables of the Ten Commandments appear and the heavenly figure coming out of the sapphire blue heaven is portrayed as a young man. Did the artist want to indicate that the new commandment of love, given by Jesus (John 13:34), rather than the Torah in stone tablets, is now put into our hearts by the Spirit? The second Old Testament story recalls the fire from heaven that vindicated the prophet Elijah in his confrontation with the false prophets (1 Kings 18:20-40). This prefiguration of Pentecost emphasizes the discerning and judging function of God's Spirit. There are evil spirits and false prophets in this world which must be confronted.

The central New Testament scene shows the Spirit descending in the form of a dove that actually pierces into the head of Mary. Apostles and people present with her all receive the Spirit, symbolized by a flame. The dove does not appear in Luke's account of Acts 2, but it is often used in art to convey the gift of the Spirit. It links Pentecost with the baptism of Jesus. Other medieval portrayals represent the Spirit with a multitude of rays of light coming out of God's hand. Already in the earliest known visual interpretation of Pentecost, that of the Mesopotamian Rabula codex of 586, Mary stands in the centre of the apostles, symbolizing the church. This became the dominant visual representation in the Western church.

Fig. 5: Pentecost

Different early portrayals, mainly from the East, show the apostles sitting with scrolls or books in their hands. Instead of Mary a throne appears with an open Bible on which stands the dove. This intimate link between God's Spirit and the scriptures is portrayed in the 9th-century Chludoff Psalter (*Fig. 5*). Streams of light from heaven touch the flames on the heads of the apostles. The classic Eastern Orthodox icon of Pentecost also does not include Mary (*Plate VIII*). There the Spirit descends on eight of the apostles, associated with the four evangelists. They sit in a harmonious community in the form of a horseshoe around a dark cave. Out of the darkness comes an old man with a royal crown, dressed in a red garment and holding a white cloth containing 12 scrolls. An inscription identifies this symbolic figure as the "cosmos",

Plate VIII: "The Descent of the Holy Spirit", egg tempera on wood, Russian, Novgorod school, 15th century

personifying the peoples of the world who now come out of darkness because they have received the gospel testimonies. Here it is not the world that surrounds the church but the apostles and evangelists who surround the world in prayer. It is only a pity that Mary of Magdala, the first witness of the risen Jesus, does not sit among them.

However strange the *Biblia Pauperum* with its typology and other Western and Eastern Pentecost iconography may look to modern viewers, it visualizes essential biblical affirmations about God's Spirit. She (in Hebrew both the Spirit and Wisdom are feminine) is related to the beginning and end of creation and history. She is the life-giving and renewing power. The people of Israel and the Christian community are given the energy of this divine wind so that the cosmos may have light and life.

The Spirit bodily present

It seems as if the Spirit, so mightily present in the act of creation and somewhat erratically also in the history and prophecy of the people of Israel, is suddenly concentrated in only one person. According to Luke's testimony, Jesus himself claimed so during his programmatic announcement in the synagogue of Nazareth: "The Spirit of the Lord is upon me, because he has anointed me to bring good news to the poor. He has sent me to proclaim release to the captives and recovery of sight to the blind, to let the oppressed go free, to proclaim the year of the Lord's favour" (4:18ff.). Jesus applies this prophecy about the messianic time, taken mainly from Isaiah 61, to himself. Then he makes what must be the shortest sermon in history: "Today this scripture has been fulfilled in your hearing."

The Spirit used to come over the prophets of the Hebrew scriptures suddenly and unexpectedly, allowing them to say and do strange and often shocking things in the name of God. As we saw in the first chapter of these reflections, this also happened to Jesus. Yet here, Luke testifies, something more takes place. In Jesus, God's Spirit was corporeally present. This is signified to us in the childhood stories by the affirmation that the Spirit begot Jesus and it is confirmed by what happened at the Jordan: "When Jesus also had been baptized and was praying, the heaven was opened, and the Holy Spirit descended upon him in bodily form like a dove. And a voice came from heaven, 'You are my Son, the Beloved; with you I am well pleased'"(3:21ff.). God's Spirit dwells and acts in Jesus. First Jesus, "full of the Holy Spirit", confronts the devil during 40 days in the desert. The battle that is joined between the destructive forces of evil and the healing, re-creating power of God leads to the climax of the passion stories and the crucifixion.

Luke insisted more strongly than the other evangelists on the action of the Spirit, but also in his gospel Jesus says little about this subject. Once, when a Samaritan village did not welcome the itinerant company, the disciples wanted to call on the judgment fire to destroy the settlement. Jesus rebuked them strongly and said (in a not well attested addition to 9:55): "You do not know what spirit you are of, for the Son of Man has not come to destroy the lives of human beings but to save them." This may throw light on another harsh and difficult saying: "And everyone who speaks a word against the Son of Man [that is against Jesus himself] will be forgiven; but whoever blasphemes against the Holy Spirit will not be forgiven" (12:10). Jesus does not force anyone to accept and to love him. But whoever blasphemes, who wickedly depraves and resists God's purpose of healing and recreating true life through the Spirit, is abandoned to the cycle of self-destruction. If Jesus actually uttered such a saying, this is probably its original meaning. By understanding it as a warning against baptized believers who renounce their faith, later interpreters limited God's cause to that of the Christians and the churches. This led to a judgmental chasing of heretics, to excommunications and various forms of inquisition.

"Filled with the power of the Spirit", Jesus started his work in Galilee, describing through parables the coming of God's kingdom and continuing the confrontation with evil spirits by exorcisms and healing. Never, though, are miracles and acts of healing described as a direct result of the Spirit.

What brings healing is belief in Jesus, his touch and his very presence. Wherever he restored, "by the finger of God", sick bodies and minds, he showed that God's kingdom was coming and that God's power was at work (11:20). The Spirit in Jesus relates more to his prophetic proclamation than to his miracles.

It is significant that, before Easter, the only promise given to the disciples that the Spirit will assist them concerns what they are to say when they are accused because of their testimony. The Spirit will become energy for the disciples only after the Pentecost. They are encouraged to pray and ask for the gift of the Spirit but, unlike Jesus himself, they do not already "rejoice in the Holy Spirit" (10:21, 11:13). We must therefore turn now to Luke's second volume, which could well be called "the Acts of the risen and ascended Lord through the Holy Spirit".

The Spirit of the frontier

After Jesus' resurrection the messianic age prophesied in the book of Isaiah has not fully arrived. At the beginning of Acts the risen Lord continues to speak "about the kingdom of God" which is still to come. In the very last verse of Acts we meet the imprisoned apostle Paul in Rome, still "proclaiming the kingdom of God and teaching about the Lord Jesus Christ with all boldness". To the proclaimed message belongs not only the announcement of the coming kingdom but also what has already happened through the death and resurrection of Jesus, the Messiah. Thus, in connection with Philip's evangelizing work in Samaria, Luke says that he "was proclaiming the good news about the kingdom of God and the name of Jesus Christ" (Acts 8:12). The journey on the edge between this world and time and the breaking in of God's kingdom continues. What, then, does the gift of the Spirit change? How is the post-Pentecost situation different from the pre-Pentecost one?

Under the impact of the Spirit the early church learned to see that Jesus of Nazareth had significance far beyond Palestine and beyond the initial decades of the first century AD.

Matthew had started the genealogy of Jesus from Abraham and the patriarchs of the Jewish people onwards. Luke traces Jesus' origin back to "Adam, son of God". Jesus here takes up and renews what began with the first human beings created as man and woman in the image of God. In the gospel itself Jesus is not called "the new Adam" or "the image of God", but this understanding underlies what Luke writes and it has much to do with the Spirit dwelling in Jesus. The Holy Spirit thus expands the horizon of time and the earth, both backward to the origins and forward to the end. The mighty wind brings movement. The last promise the risen Lord gives to his disciples is a universal commission: "You will receive power when the Holy Spirit has come upon you; and you will be my witnesses in Jerusalem, in all Judea and Samaria, and to the ends of the earth" (Acts 1:8).

Pentecost has often been called the birthday of the church but this does not correspond entirely with what Luke tells us in Acts. True, believers now receive the name "Christians" for the first time (Acts 11:26) and local communities of such believers are sometimes called an *ekklesia*, a church in a given place. If, however, we examine all the passages about the Spirit in the Acts we discover that almost all of them concern prophetic proclamation on the frontier between church and world. Unlike Paul's letters, where the Spirit and community (*koinonia*) are intimately linked, Luke never uses this term in connection with the Holy Spirit. Nor does he make a direct link between the Spirit and the breaking of the bread.

Strange things happen on the frontier. The story of the first Christian Pentecost relates the rush of a violent wind, the tongues of fire and the speaking in tongues, which is interpreted as a language or a hearing miracle: everyone who is endowed with the Spirit understands what is being said. The language confusion at the tower of Babel is being overcome. Healing, visions, dreams, the shaking of the earth and prophecies occur where the Spirit breaks in. Such more extraordinary phenomena should not astonish those who have read the gospels and have not watered down the extraordinary things Jesus did and said. When the Spirit blows into the life of people and communities there will be movement and change. The history of Christian mission is full of events similar to those recounted in Acts. Such remarkable and often only short-term manifestations of the Spirit occur especially among first generation Christians. What does Luke tell us about the more constant and enduring impact of Pentecost in the lives of early Christians?

Usually the gift of the Spirit is linked to baptism, a typical frontier experience and a rite of passage. Nothing about baptism is regulated as yet and the situation remains fluid. There are those, like the Jewish-Christian teacher Apollos, who had been instructed in the Way but knew only of the baptism of John the Baptist (18:25, 19:2ff.). Others received the Spirit but were not yet baptized (10:44ff.). Did the apostles and 120 believers mentioned in Acts 1 ever receive water baptism? Does water baptism and/or the laying-on of hands confer the Spirit? There clearly is nothing automatic about these relationships. The Spirit is given for the whole life of believers but in certain situations it can be given anew (4:31).

More important than the rite of baptism, according to Luke, is the intimate link between the reception of the Spirit and prayer and the link with conversion and belief. What the Spirit confers is the courage and boldness of faith *(parresia)*, which frees believers and enables them to become witnesses to the risen Lord through word, deed and life. This boldness comes from the fact that the risen and ascended Jesus is present through the Spirit. What was said in Chapter 3 about the transparent cross and transparent reality can become an actual experience through the Spirit. The eyes, the mouths and the understanding of the witnesses are being opened. The martyr Stephen even saw the heavens opened, "filled with the Holy Spirit, he saw the glory of God and Jesus standing at the right hand of God" (7:55ff.).

A turning point

Luke does not give us a doctrine about the Holy Spirit. Rather, he tells us stories about how the Spirit moves and acts. One of the most crucial ones, the longest story in Acts, is the meeting of the Roman officer Cornelius with the apostle Peter; both men were met by the Spirit (Acts 10:1-11:18). It may be that two different traditions are behind the present text, one about a debate among Jewish Christians over what is clean and unclean and the other about how Cornelius received the Spirit. With his narrator's skill, Luke has interwoven the two into a drama with seven acts, summarized in *Worksheet C* (pp. 96-97). We will concentrate mainly on the fifth and sixth scenes, which are quoted in the worksheet.

Peter's speech in the house of Cornelius follows a pattern that is also found in other apostolic proclamations in Acts. The message Peter gives connects with what has already happened to his audience. Unexpected events have already opened the ears of his listeners and awoken their curiosity. Missionary proclamation does not start with a biblical text or a transmitted doctrine but begins by referring to a personal or corporate experience. In this case it is what Peter himself has just learned from the vision he received in Joppa. The original text of 10:34f. could be paraphrased in this way: God does not judge by outward appearance and shows no partiality. In every nation those who stand in awe before God and work for justice are acceptable to him.

This opening is followed by the main gospel message about what God has done through Jesus the Messiah. It can function as a summary of much of what has been written so far in these reflections about the Way. If, for instance, we compare it with Paul's teaching and later doctrinal Christian statements, we can discern several emphases that are typical of Luke's testimony. Here the earthly life and the healing work of Jesus of Nazareth before his crucifixion and resurrection are fully part of the apostolic message. The anointment by the Spirit and God's presence with Jesus is stressed. The crucifixion, the "hanging on the tree", is reported without any further interpretation and the accent lies more on the resurrection and the presence of the risen Lord, testified to by the apostles. Jesus is seen as the one who brings peace and well-being through his struggle with demonic powers. He is also proclaimed as the judge of the living and the dead. The note of urgency and the coming critical end of history are expressed, but the final emphasis lies on forgiveness, as it does in Luke's account of the crucifixion. Only at that point, when speaking about the forgiveness and acceptance in the name of Jesus, is there a reference to the testimony of the Hebrew prophets.

Then Peter is interrupted. The Spirit falls on all who hear the apostolic message. Neither the laying-on of hands nor the rite of water baptism are performed before the Spirit appears. There is neither an account of a preceding conversion nor an outspoken confession by the ones who are "baptized" by the Spirit. It is as if the apostolic proclamation triggers the event. True, Cornelius was prepared to listen with expectancy. As a "god-fearer" in contact with the synagogue, he was even supposed to have already heard something about Jesus. But the Spirit comes suddenly, with the immediate manifestation of speaking in tongues and praising God. To the astonishment of the Jewish Christians who are present, the Spirit falls beyond the frontiers of what for them was the church. It falls "even on Gentiles"! Peter draws this conclusion: Let the uncircumcised, too, be baptized by water. The actual performance of the rite is not even mentioned.

For the early church, and for Luke, this first incorporation of a whole group of Gentiles into the Christian community became a decisive turning point. The last scene of the story, now with Jerusalem as the stage, reveals only the beginning of the impact that the Spirit's crossing of frontiers began to have on the further history of the Way. The apostles and believers of the mother church in Jerusalem did not dare to challenge the actual coming of the Spirit on the Gentiles, lest they would blaspheme the Spirit. They did, however, express serious reservations about Peter's eating with the uncircumcised. Nevertheless, they acknowledged that "God has given even to the Gentiles the repentance that leads to life". It is significant that they spoke only about the Gentiles' change of thinking, the outsiders' conversion. They had not yet realized that the Spirit was also prompting them to go through a change of thinking, a conversion in the mother church. This would create many further discussions and tensions, as Acts 15 and the letters of Paul document.

Discerning where God's Spirit moves

In this story we discover the great variety of agents God uses to realize his plan. At the beginning stands a "god-fearer", a praying man in awe before God. During the first century Christian mission advanced essentially in the border area between the synagogue and the non-Jewish sympathizers of Old Testament faith. The angel of God meets Cornelius. Angels in the Bible are not sweet, winged creatures flying through the air but human agents with a message from God. (In Christian iconography winged angels appeared only from the 4th century onwards.) In Joppa a trance, a vision and an unspecified voice puzzle the other protagonist of the story, the apostle Peter. He is then told directly by the Spirit to receive the people sent from Caesaria and to accompany them. Meanwhile Cornelius has set the stage for the apostle to proclaim the message, but soon the Holy Spirit intervenes directly once again.

Such an unsystematic plurality of agents characterizes the whole of the book of Acts. Behind it all stands the risen Lord and it is impossible to make a distinction between God's, Christ's and the Spirit's work. There is clearly a deep conviction that a plan of salvation is being realized in people's lives. This plan is interwoven with world history, neither totally separated from it nor totally identified with it. The key for understanding this divine design is contained in the apostolic proclamation that announces forgiveness and calls for a new way of thinking and living, a conversion. People and groups galvanized by the interventions of the risen Lord or the Spirit play a role in the realization of the divine plan, even though they often do not clearly understand it. A decision taken in prayer and "resolved in the Spirit" may be challenged by prophetic utterances also given "through the Spirit". This happens with regard to Paul's decision to go to Jerusalem (19:21, 21:4). The God of the Bible remains strange, often hidden and ever surprising.

* * *

If, like Peter and Cornelius and so many others in Luke's testimonies, we want to walk on the Way, we must attempt to discern where the Spirit moves today. Otherwise the dangerous currents of the present age might carry us away. Discernment means first of all to persevere in the prayer: "Come, Creator Spirit!" We can help that discernment by trying to envisage a metaphor for the energy of the Spirit in today's world. My attempt to weave a tapestry for Pentecost (*Fig. 6*) shows a red comet erupting into currents that are all flowing towards the left, and drawing them to the right. What would be your metaphor for Pentecost?

Fig. 6

The page of the medieval *Biblia Pauperum* looks back from Pentecost to Old Testament stories and prophecies. We might turn the perspective around and look forward from Pentecost. Where has the Spirit acted in events in church and world history? How does the Spirit impact on your own life's story? Who are the prophets with deep insight in our own days? Readers may want to end this reflection by conceiving a Pentecost page for today's *Biblia Pauperum*:

- Find for the centre of the page a metaphor for the Spirit, preferably not using the traditional ones of the dove and the flame.
- Indicate with a sentence or a drawing two events from recent history where you are convinced that the Holy Spirit was at work.
- Put around your Pentecost metaphor the portraits of four people who, in the last few decades, have made truly prophetic acts, found prophetic insights and announced them with boldness.

5. The Great Advent

A crown of fir branches plaited anew each year by mother's hands. On it four candles, but only one of them lit on the first Sunday of Advent. A week later two candles are lit together, then three and finally all four on the fourth Sunday of Advent. This is how I remember the weeks before Christmas in my childhood. In our family we have kept up this custom of the advent crown with its symbolism of growing light in the dark evenings of the northern hemisphere winter. Meanwhile Christmas is being ever more commercialized and I doubt whether many of our own children and grandchildren will remember the Advent crown as a symbol of Christian hope and awaiting.

Advertising, promoting new things and experiences, creates the wish to have it all and have it at once. The hectic acceleration of life threatens to affect more and more people and at times even the recurring cycle of the ecclesiastical year seems to be caught in this rush. Is it possible to hope ever again for the child born more than 2000 years ago? Can we, year after year, participate fully in the events celebrated on Good Friday and Easter? By walking on the Way do we not risk walking in a circle? Perhaps we have to learn anew from the Hebrew prophets what the great Awaiting, the great adventure of Advent really means. Indeed, for the early Christians Advent did not refer to the weeks before Christmas but to the waiting for the *parousia*, for the coming of Christ in glory and for the establishment of God's kingdom on earth.

Millennia of waiting

For three millennia the Israelites have been waiting for the day of the Lord. Of course there was the exodus and the entry into the Promised Land with a partly peaceful and partly military occupation of Palestine. Some thought that the kingship of David would bring the promised rest, peace and well-being. But the waiting continued as one Davidic king after another failed to fulfil these expectations. Then the Assyrians, later the Babylonians and finally the Romans dispersed God's chosen people into successive exiles. The Jews of the diaspora never tired of saying at the close of their Passover feast, "Next year in Jerusalem!" When, after the great exile, the state of Israel was established and fought for, the hopes of many Jews ran high again. But anyone who reads the prophecies of the Hebrew scripture and the daily newspapers side by side knows that this state is not yet the fulfilment of biblical hopes. Can Jerusalem become the city of shalom, the city of peace, if it is partly based on injustice to the Arabs, also "children of Abraham", who have lived in Palestine for more than 13 centuries?

The prophets taught that the way to the expected day of the Lord and to universal peace would pass through Jerusalem. Isaiah announced: "Many peoples shall come and say, 'Come, let us go up to the mountain of the Lord... that he may teach us his ways and that we may walk in his paths.' For out of Zion shall go forth instruction [torah], and the word of the Lord from Jerusalem." Peoples "shall beat their swords into ploughshares and their spears into pruning hooks; nation shall not lift up sword against nation, neither shall they learn war any more" (Isa. 2:2-4). The same prophet re-envisaged kingship: a future Davidic king would come, "a Prince of Peace", endowed with God's spirit and wisdom, in whose reign the poor will be judged with justice and the wolf will live with the lamb (Isa. 9:6ff., 11:1ff.).

During the Babylonian exile, when Davidic kingship had failed miserably, another great prophet arose, usually called the Second Isaiah. His oracles are collected in Isaiah 40-55. He dared to affirm that, in his historic situation, not a Davidic king but the Persian conqueror Cyrus was God's agent and God's anointed one. Cyrus would make possible a new exodus and enable the exiled Israelites to return to Jerusalem. This prophet of the exile, later so often quoted and alluded to in the testimonies of Luke, clearly proclaimed God's sovereignty over the whole of history and the whole of creation. Although he did not play down the coming divine judgment for both the Israelites and the nations, his main message was one of consolation and hope. The Israelites' particular status of election and their special covenant relationship with God were maintained, but the real purpose of this election was now strongly emphasized: the elect people are called to become God's servant and to be "a light to the nations". Second Isaiah's poems about God's servant portray this task, whether they originally refer to the whole people, to a remnant or to a coming servant figure and suffering prophet.

Many Israelites did not return from Babylon and Egypt and those who did come back faced disappointment. Life continued around the rebuilt temple of Jerusalem, the keeping of the sabbath and the study of the Torah, but much of Second Isaiah's vision for his people remained unfulfilled. The waiting never ceased. Among the various prophecies collected in the closing chapters of the book of Isaiah one finds the words of hope taken up by later New Testament testimonies. After harsh pronouncements of judgment for those who do not respond to the divine calling, God gives a promise: "I am about to create new heavens and a new earth; the former things shall not be remembered or come to mind. But be glad and rejoice forever in what I am creating; for I am about to create Jerusalem as a joy... No more shall there be in it an infant that lives but a few days, or an old person who does not live out a life-time... They shall build houses and inhabit them; they shall plant vineyards and eat their fruit... The wolf and the lamb shall feed together" (Isa. 65:17-25).

Here we are in the border area between prophetic announcements and apocalyptic visions. Prophecy had ended with Haggai, Zechariah and Malachi. The sages had begun to reflect on the origin, order and end of the created world and about the course and purpose of history. Using as a basis such wisdom speculations and the former prophetic announcements, the apocalyptic visionaries began to interpret the history of their time. They saw an inescapable sequence of human empires leading up to a catastrophic climax. They discerned signs of the coming end and began to calculate when it would come. In the visions of Daniel and Henoch this drama of the end is vividly described. There we find, too, the enigmatic announcement of the coming of the "Son of

Man". Such high hopes accompanied the Maccabean revolt, but the attempt to re-establish David's reign lasted less than 100 years (142-63 BC). A century later, in AD 70, the Jewish war against Rome led to the destruction of Jerusalem and its temple.

Meanwhile John the Baptist's call to conversion and Jesus' announcement and anticipation of God's kingdom had come and gone. The continuing Jesus movement was still seen partly as a Jewish sect, but Christians were already being excluded from the synagogues. Soon the ways of rabbinical Judaism and what Luke called the Way were separating. Jews could not see in Jesus the expected Messiah and they read the Hebrew scriptures differently from the early Christians and the authors of the New Testament. So the waiting for the day of the Lord continued. For the Jews only? We are back to John the Baptist's question to Jesus: "Are you the one who is to come, or shall we wait for another?" In order to see how early Christians lived with the fact that God's kingdom had not come as soon as they had hoped, we turn again to Luke.

The coming of God's kingdom

In a sense, of course, the expected kingdom is already manifest in Jesus. Luke reports the incident when a Pharisee asked Jesus when God's kingdom was coming. He received the following answer: "The kingdom of God is not coming with things that can be observed; nor will they say, 'Look, here it is!' or 'There it is!' For, in fact, the kingdom of God is among you" (Luke 17:20ff., cf. the "upon you" in 11:20). This warning begins a passage in which Luke has collected what Jesus said to his disciples about his coming. There will be false messengers who may mislead the disciples to believe that the day of the Son of Man has come. For the moment this Son of Man was indeed present in Jesus of Nazareth, but in the form of a human servant and prophet, as the one who first "must endure much suffering and be rejected by this generation". This should not cause the disciples to be like the people in the time of Noah and of Lot, thoughtlessly eating and drinking without considering God's intervention. The end will come as the lightning flashes and it will lead to a surprising separation of people. At that future time the Son of Man will be revealed in his glory. His coming (in a parallel text Matthew uses the term *parousia*) will be obvious to all.

Jesus was already on the way up to Jerusalem and to the cross when he taught in this way about the kingdom. Then came the crucifixion, the resurrection and what Luke tells us about the ascension. Would this initiate the hoped-for coming of the Messiah in glory and the establishment of God's kingdom?

The first account of Jesus being carried up into heaven (Luke 24:50ff.) is set in a strongly liturgical frame and told with great expectancy. The gospel began with an unfinished temple worship when Zechariah, struck dumb, could not pronounce the blessing. Now the risen Jesus completes that service, giving the blessing while ascending. This happens not in the temple but outside Jerusalem. Having received the blessing, the disciples respond with joyful worship.

The second account of ascension is revealing in its rich symbolism and metaphors (Acts 1:6ff.). In antiquity and in biblical thinking numbers are not simply arithmetical measures but symbolic pointers. For instance, 40 often indicates a time of testing and a preparatory period for a new stage of life. Noah spent 40 days in the ark, Moses stayed for 40 days on Mount Sinai and the people of the exodus erred 40 years in the desert. Elijah walked 40 days in the wilderness to meet God at Horeb and Jesus was 40 days fasting and being tempted in the desert. Now Luke tells us that 40 days after the resurrection Jesus was lifted up. The scene recalls the story when Elijah was carried away into heaven just like that other hero of faith, Henoch, who plays such a great role in the apocalyptic writings. Luke adds that the ascension took place on the Mount of Olives which, according to prophecies of Zechariah, will be the place of the final cataclysm and of the establishment of God's kingdom.

In biblical language, "heaven" is neither the sky nor an especially holy and divine area above. That type of heaven (in Hebrew it is usually plural) was created like the earth and will need to be re-created. In antiquity the sun and the moon were often seen as divine, but the priestly writers of Genesis 1 placed the making of the sun and the moon only on the fourth "day". So what biblical authors call heaven – God's realm and throne – lies beyond our earth and skies. It is a metaphor for transcendence. God resides "above the heavens" (Ps. 108:5).

By his ascending the risen Jesus passes from the world that is visible to human eyes to the world where God alone rules. Ascension thus means an absence, yet an absence that allows a new type of presence, namely through the Spirit. As the disciples "were gazing up towards heaven" two messengers in white robes asked them, "Why do you stand looking up towards heaven? This Jesus, who has been taken up from you into heaven, will come in the same way as you saw him go into heaven." The disciples' task is here on earth. Here they are to be witnesses in word and deed, here they have actively to wait for the coming of Jesus and of God's kingdom.

The apostle Peter transmitted a similar message in his first public appearance after Pentecost. He had just healed a crippled beggar sitting in a gate to the temple courts. The astonished onlookers wondered where Peter's power had come from. This became the context for announcing the gospel of resurrection, here especially addressed to Jews. Placing the life and death of Jesus firmly in the history of the patriarchs, Peter presented Jesus with terms and titles from the Hebrew scriptures: the Servant of God, the Holy and Righteous One, the Author of life and a prophet like Moses. His announcement directs attention back to the prophets, forward to the promised future and to the implications that such a wide perspective has for the present day.

In the original Greek, the central part of Peter's address consists only of two long and involved sentences (Acts 3:18-21). The passage is here broken up into its separate parts and paraphrased:
1) You, fellow Jews, you know that God fulfills what he announced by the prophets of the scriptures.

2) They foretold that the expected Messiah would have to suffer among his own people (as Jesus of Nazareth, the Messiah, had indeed to suffer and be crucified right here in Jerusalem).
3) Therefore this is the time to change your thinking and turn to God.
4) Then God will wipe out your sins.
5) Moreover it means that, as a result of God's presence, the time of refreshment and ultimate healing will come.
6) This will coincide with the time when God will send Jesus, who has been predetermined for you as the Messiah.
7) This Jesus must, however, remain in heaven, in the presence of God, until the appointed time.
8) That time will be the restoration of all that the prophets have already spoken about.

This condensed passage shows us how the early Christians explained the fact that, despite the crucifixion, resurrection and ascension of Jesus, the kingdom of God had not yet fully come. Reflecting about Pentecost we saw that, through the gift of the Spirit, time and space were expanded. Just as a stone, thrown into a pond, creates ever larger ripples, so the Spirit widens the frontier between this world and the kingdom of God. What was schematically visualized in *Figure 2* (p. 12) would now have to be expanded. Further time and space would be given for repentance and forgiveness, and for being witnesses. Both the prophets and the early Christians had a strong awareness that all was not well in this world. Social sins, especially injustice and violence, and personal sins such as hypocrisy, lack of love and idolatry were squarely faced. If the hope and visions of the prophets were to become a reality, a new way of thinking, acting and turning to God was needed, both among Christians and among the nations. So the early Christians did not experience the time and space opened up by Jesus' ascension and by the gift of the Spirit only as an absence. They also saw them as an opportunity and a grace, despite the further waiting and despite persecutions.

The hope remained alive. It was not only the prophetic promises of the past but also the hoped for "times of refreshment" that made a strong impact on present life. The word translated as "refreshment" comes from medical language describing the easing of pain. Here it stands for the end times and the establishment of God's kingdom. The early Christians knew the face of Jesus, the Son of Man, in his very human, servant guise as the suffering prophet. They could therefore await with confidence his coming as the Son of Man in glory. The ascension of their Lord and the time before his *parousia* was seen as part of God's plan; it stood under the divine "must".

It is significant that the New Testament makes no clear distinction between a first and a second coming of Jesus. His advent remains a future event and is never called a "return" or a "coming again". Only in the latter half of the 2nd century did the Christian apologist Justin begin to apply the term *parousia* also to the incarnation of Jesus. Consequently he then spoke about a "second coming". From then on this non-biblical term became current among theologians and gradually the weeks before Christmas were called Advent.

The time of universal restoration

What did Peter exactly mean when, in his proclamation to the Jews, he used the expression "the restoration of all" (*apokatastasis panton*)? This is the only place in the whole Bible where the term occurs. Some interpreters relate it only to the fulfilment of the prophecies given to the Israelites and understand it to refer to the future destiny of the Jewish people. And at the beginning of Acts the verb from which the noun derives is indeed used in connection with Israelite hopes. The disciples there ask, "Lord, is this the time when you will restore the kingdom to Israel?" (1:6). They still misunderstand Jesus' ministry in a national-political sense. Other interpreters see in this expression a metaphor for the end of the whole cosmos and time. In Greek philosophical and astronomical literature *apokatastasis* is used to describe the re-establishment of the order of the universe. Elsewhere in biblical thinking one finds the assertion that the end will bring back the beginning, a messianic re-creation. The two interpretations, the one relating it to the destiny of the Jewish people and the one extending this restoration to the whole universe and time, are not mutually exclusive. A cosmic messianic end-time can include the re-establishment of the elect people of Israel.

On the basis of the condensed biblical text we can say no more, although many divergent and often far-fetched assertions have been made. Does *apokatastasis* mean that all will be saved, that all things will be restored to their original state and the lost paradise found? We have to acknowledge that, for many of our questions, the Bible does not provide the answer. In pondering such questions, the continuation of Luke's narrative is both relevant and intriguing. Immediately after his first public proclamation Peter had to defend himself before the Jewish authorities who asked him which power had allowed him to heal. He declared, "There is salvation in no one else [than Jesus], for there is no other name under heaven given among mortals by which we must be saved" (Acts 4:12). Such a statement should not be taken out of context, fixed as a dogma for all times and applied to people of other faiths. Peter spoke within and for a specific situation. For the early Christians no other name but Jesus' would save. According to the New Testament, Jesus is confessed as *the* Way. But what about all the people who have never known that name and that Way? The Spirit was at work long before New Testament times. Can God's Spirit not lead these fellow human beings to salvation through their scriptures and their wisdom? I believe this, although I cannot prove it from the New Testament.

The above reflections call for a comment on Christian mission. The testimony of Luke is quite clear. Mission forms an integral part of Christian faith. To be witnesses means to tell the story of the Way while attempting to walk according to that Way. The missionary frontier passes first through the witnesses themselves. They must let the Spirit convert them again and again so that what they do and say does not belie their message. Beyond the witnesses and their fellowship lies the *oikoumene*, the whole inhabited world. The witnesses are sent out "until the ends of the earth". Jesus never promised that the *oikoumene* would become Christian. The over 20 parables of Luke's gospel are not concerned with the growth of the church but, rather, teach about the critical times when God's kingdom is at hand. In connection with this coming kingdom Jesus encouraged the small group: "Do not be afraid, little flock." He even once wondered whether, at his coming, he will "find faith on earth" (Luke 12:32, 18:8). In the Acts numerical church growth is seen as the impact of the Spirit, but no full Christianization of the Roman empire is envisaged beyond the implantation of small Christian communities in the cities. Personally, I like to think of Christian world mission as analogous to the election and calling of God's people as Second Isaiah saw it: a worldwide minority meant to become a blessing, a light to the nations. Such election for a universal task is a dangerous calling and it has often led to arrogance and sinful pride. It is good, therefore, to remember that Christians, too, do not own God's kingdom and the final truth. Together with the Jewish people and with all the peoples on earth – Paul included "with the whole creation" (Rom. 8) – we still await the restoration of all.

A new heaven and a new earth

This great promise appears not only in the passage quoted earlier from the book of Isaiah. It is also the metaphor used in the last great parable of God's kingdom in the Bible, the final vision of John's Revelation (Rev. 21-22). When those who have been nurtured by the Bible consider the end of this earth and this time, the powerful images of the apocalypse begin to play like a motion picture in our minds. We see the lightning and hear the thunder. A door in the heavens is opened. The woes of those being judged and the hallelujahs of the martyrs reach our ears. Christ appears as the slaughtered, victorious Lamb. Before his throne we are invited to participate in a counter-liturgy against the glorification of the emperor and of all arrogant powerful ones. With the martyrs we are empowered to resist, to persevere and to hope against all human hope. In the last vision we glimpse the heavenly Jerusalem coming down on earth. There will be no more closed doors. Because God and the Lamb will be present there will no longer be any need for a temple. Nor will there be any more death, mourning or pain. A river flows with the water of life and on its bank grows the tree of life whose leaves are "for the healing of the nations".

Searching to express visually the great waiting for the new heaven and the new earth, I have not turned to this rich iconography of John's Revelation. There was enough apocalyptic envisioning at the recent turn of the millennium, and too often it emphasized only the catastrophes and the judgment of the end. It was marked more strongly by fear than by biblical hope. Moreover, the hoped-for end far exceeds all human imagination. So, in weaving a tapestry about waiting for the great Advent, I chose non-figurative, symbolic forms

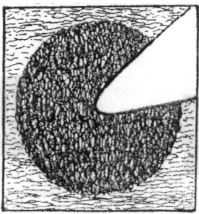

Fig. 7

and colours (*Fig. 7*): a circle made with thick threads of wool in the three basic colours of red, blue and yellow, from which all colours stem. The parabola that breaks open that closed circle and reaches out into the infinite is woven with thin, pure silk. Thus the hope for a new heaven and a new earth opens up our life to transcendence. Like Easter faith, the great Awaiting can make the cross transparent and, within human realities, give us glimpses of the reality of God.

How could Christians keep that parabola open, even when the expected establishment of God's kingdom was delayed from one generation to the other? Many, of course, grew weak in their waiting. They began to identify the church with God's kingdom, especially when the churches became earthly powers. The great Old Testament promises and Jesus' proclamation about the kingdom were narrowed down to apply mainly to individual believers or to a life in the hereafter. The cosmic significance of Jesus' death and resurrection, the great biblical hope for a new heaven and a new earth, became dim. Good Friday and Easter were often seen primarily in relation only to the believer's own salvation and resurrection after death.

A seldom-read part of the New Testament, the short second letter of Peter, has some striking parallels with what is written about the expectation of the end in Luke's gospel and the Acts. It shows how Christians continued to hope for the day of the Lord, the great Advent. This intriguing document brings us to the border period between the apostolic age and the church of the early 2nd century. It is probably the latest of all New Testament writings. Because of the late date and the long controversy about whether 2 Peter could become part of the New Testament, most present interpreters believe that its author was not the apostle Peter. And this assumption is confirmed by the document's peculiar vocabulary, style and content. The best hypothesis is that an unknown author wrote this farewell letter in the form of a "Petrine" testament, a literary genre well known among Jews and Christians of that time.

Here we are no longer at the missionary frontier, as in the book of Acts, but in a divided Christian community. There was a danger that believers were being led astray by what the author calls the heresy of false prophets and teachers who "malign the way of truth" and have departed from "the way of justice". Therefore the testament has a fiercely polemic tone, especially in its second chapter, which uses much of the letter of Jude written earlier (one of the many biblical chapters I do not particularly like!). The testament's main purpose, though, is not polemic but pastoral. The author wants to strengthen his listeners in their hope so that they may "grow in grace and knowledge of our Lord and Saviour Jesus Christ".

The very question that has accompanied us throughout these reflections, namely the delay of the coming of God's kingdom and of the *parousia* of Jesus Christ, is explicitly taken up here. The false teachers asked sceptically, "Where is the promise of his coming? For ever since our ancestors died, all things continue as they were from the beginning of creation!" (3:4). They had apparently given up the prophetic promises and the biblical hope. At home in the closed circle of this world and time, they lived a futile, self-indulgent life, as if no judgment would come and as if they were not responsible to their Creator. Refuting their doubts about prophetic promises and their denial of the coming *parousia*, the testament of "Peter" makes the following points.

First, in a time when the apostles have died and the oral tradition about Jesus is either being lost or overgrown with fanciful teachings, the author specifies what holds true authority for Christian faith. The guiding authority is now to be found in the prophetic Old Testament, the commandments of the Lord and the written testimonies of the apostles (the letters of Peter and Paul are explicitly mentioned). The author thus anticipates what, after his time, gradually became the canon of the Bible for Christians. It is these scriptures, coming from God "by men and women moved by the Holy Spirit", which must now continue to refresh the memory of believers. It is noteworthy that there is no specific mention of a Petrine office or the teaching ministry of bishops.

The content of Christian faith is presupposed, for the readers have already "received faith" and "are established in truth". Only one gospel story is mentioned: the transfiguration of Jesus where, in the midst of his earthly life, he appeared in his glory. That manifestation is seen as an anticipation of the *parousia* and a guarantee for the fulfilment of prophecies. Also, the stories of the flood in Noah's time and what happened to the cities of Sodom and Gomorrah are recalled. They show that God is free to destroy what was created and create it anew by a divine word.

In connection with the coming judgment the author takes up a Jewish apocalyptic expectation, taught also by some philosophers of the time, namely that the heavens and the earth will be destroyed by a cosmic fire. Contrary to the apocalypses of his time, he does not expand on such imagery but looks beyond the judgment to the promised new creation. The accent is strongly on the ethical conduct that biblical hope implies for the present time.

The main message for those who have become uncertain in their hope is concisely stated: "Do not ignore this one fact, beloved, that with the Lord one day is like a thousand years, and a thousand years are like one day. The Lord is not slow about his promise, as some think of slowness, but is patient with you, not wanting any to perish, but all to come to repentance" (3:8-9). Old Testament passages from Psalm 90:4, Habakkuk 2:3 and Isaiah 55:8ff. are recalled. God's time and eyes, God's thoughts and ways cannot be measured by human means. A fundamental reversal of perspective is required. The waiting for the *parousia* may well seem long to the believers, but the decisive waiting is that of God. In patience God waits for the repentance of all. History continues because of this long-suffering, great-hearted and patient divine waiting so that God's creatures may become what they are meant to be. For the author the "all" may refer only to the Christians he addressed. Yet in this respect God's thinking is probably more all-embracing than we generally assume.

* * *

The sceptical teachers were hardly won over by this message and I doubt that today's sceptics will be convinced. The stated arguments can be written off as naïve wishful thinking. I have, though, nothing better to offer for the present time.

Like the visionary of John's Revelation and the author of the testament of "Peter", we live in an apocalyptic situation. Our universe has been vastly expanded. Living on a planet that turns around the sun we know that beyond the solar system lies a wide and unfathomable space. What is at stake for us is life and survival on this planet earth. For many this means simply their families' and their own individual span of life before death. Through great scientific discoveries and their technological applications, life has changed far beyond what could have been imagined only a few generations ago. Some see in this change thrilling opportunities and progress. Others warn that the future holds widespread ecological catastrophes, an absolutist dominance by the economy, a growing generalized violence and unfettered genetic engineering. All of us have to face this ambiguous future, corporately with regard to life on this earth and personally with the certainty of death.

We can face such an uncertain future in two different ways. The first approach takes its starting point from present realities. We then plan, work, fear and hope according to *the probable future*. The second approach starts from promises given and trusted. We then plan, work, suffer, wait and hope for *the promised future*. Clearly these two approaches are in tension with one another but need not be mutually exclusive. Today's world emphasizes strongly the wisdom of planning and forecasting on the basis of the present realities. Much of the New Testament emphasizes the adventure of faith, starting with the divine promises.

In the light of past history, present uncertainties and with a view to the coming end the author of 2 Peter challenges us. He asks, "What sort of persons ought you to be in leading lives of holiness and godliness, waiting for and hastening the coming of the day of God?" (3:11ff.). This leads to the great affirmation of hope:

"In accordance with God's promise,
we wait for new heavens and a new earth,
where righteousness/justice is at home."

Epilogue

The journey continues. There is still life on this earth. Human beings still search for meaning. The spiral of the ecclesiastical year can refocus the attention of Christians on Jesus and the great Advent. Are we, under God's patience, embarking on another millennium or a new long series of millennia, of which we shall experience only the very beginning?

"Waiting for and hastening the coming of the day of God." In old age the waiting part of it becomes a daily exercise: waiting during sleepless hours for the coming of the morning. Waiting for the last great rite of passage, the mystery of death. For many this inescapably approaching decay of one's bodily and mental forces is a fearful experience. If it is accepted as part of the great Advent it can become also a confident waiting, a gradual giving of oneself.

The hastening part has always intrigued me. Some translate this rare expression only with "earnestly desiring", but in the above quoted passage from Second Peter it probably means more. The few other occurrences of the verb appear only in Luke's writing. The shepherds in the field hasten to see the newborn child. Zacchaeus hastens down from his observation post on the sycamore tree to come into the presence of Jesus and to prepare a feast. Can the faithfulness of our waiting for a new heaven and a new earth and our earnest desire to seek the presence of Jesus have an impact on world history, shortening or prolonging its course? Jewish rabbis believed that their people's faithfulness to God's calling could shorten or delay the coming of the messianic age. Also, in the Acts, the realization of God's plan for the salvation of the world is intimately interwoven with the life and faithfulness of the witnesses.

Leaving such speculations we turn again to what Luke tells us about the Way. Of course, we will also have to listen to the other witnesses in the New Testament, and in some circumstances they speak to us more strongly than Luke does. I am convinced, though, that, especially today, the third gospel and the Acts have much to teach us. Those who are involved in struggles of faith more crucial than mine will gain from Luke further directions and encouragement for walking on the Way. Here, in a nutshell, is how he has spoken to me.

The Jesus we meet through Luke's eyes is a very earthly one. He comes to us into our daily lives and seeks us when we feel at a loss. Knowing our longings and our shortcomings, he prays for us, forgives our sins, converts and heals us. In the midst of the emergency situation of God's kingdom at hand he has time for us and shows a particular concern for those in need, for the poor.

According to Luke, Jesus does not accomplish this work of salvation through a vicarious sacrifice. (The evangelist may have feared that the language of sacrifice and substitution could mislead us on a way of cheap grace, away from our own responsibilities.) Rather, Jesus enters into our human condition, innocently suffering there as the Just One and liberating us from networks of evil. His way of salvation is the restoration of health, joy and peace. The fact that Luke spoke so often about healing does not prove that he was a physician. He did not use more medical terms than were current among writers of his time and culture. The insistence on the restoration of physical and mental health truly reflects what Luke had heard about Jesus and what he saw happening in the early church. He saw healing as *the* sign of God's kingdom coming upon us.

An important part of the saving process is the way in which the risen Jesus associates believers with his own ministry, initiating them into *his* pattern of life. He joins them together in an odd community and sends them out to serve God's plan. They are called into a frontier existence, ready to catch up with the new advances of the Spirit into the *oikoumene*, witnessing boldly. We have seen how Luke's testimony opens up vast perspectives of space and time. According to the original meaning of the word *oikoumene* Luke was, par excellence, the ecumenical witness, teaching us not only *what* to witness but also *how* to witness.

Luke is rightly known as the theologian of salvation history, the skilful writer nurtured by the Greek translation of the Old Testament, but he also was an excellent story-teller. Adapting his style to his audience, he knew to portray the actors with a few telling details, and that is why his gospel and apostle stories stick in the mind and memory. He started the tradition of narrative Christian theology. From the 6th century AD onwards the legend developed that Luke was a painter and in medieval art the third evangelist is sometimes shown painting Mary and the child Jesus. There is no historical basis for this legend, but one can well imagine why Luke became the patron saint of the painters' guilds. He knew how to paint with words. He had an eye for symbolism, for instance that of significant times and places, and he was sensitive to metaphorical language, as the accounts of Jesus' ascension and the Pentecost show. The childhood narratives include hymns that have since become treasured parts of church liturgy and are now prayed and sung in all continents. It would not be surprising if a legend about Luke as a musician had also developed. Indeed, he was not primarily a theologian (if this is understood to mean systematic reflection and exposition of doctrines); he was a theo-poet.

Luke probably never sat before a loom, weaving in between his travels and his writing. Or might he have done so? The author of Acts implies that he accompanied the apostle Paul on stretches of the missionary journeys. He also reports that Paul was a tent-maker from Cilicia, a region well known for its weaving of rough fabrics with goat hair. Did Luke sit with Paul at the loom? Nobody knows, but I like to imagine him doing so. If he had, this theo-poet would certainly have discovered the deep symbolism of weaving. He might have seen the whole *oikoumene* as a great frame and the many cultures as a magnificent assortment of differently coloured threads. I imagine him working on the still unfinished large tapestry of world history, weaving into it the parts that hold the loose fabric together: small communities of hope and healing as the Jesus movement and the churches are called to be. Luke did not claim to know the final pattern of this unfinished tapestry, yet he would have seen the symbolism of the cross, that of life given for creating interconnection and community. He knew that, to continue the work, many more crosses are needed, many more given lives.

Appendix

It always is more interesting and instructive to make a discovery for oneself than simply to read what others have written. Therefore here are **some suggestions for Bible study leaders** about how they might proceed in order to examine, with a small group, some of the key texts reflected upon in this book.

For each of the following studies allow a *time span* of about 1 ¾ or 2 hours. Plan for (1) the *opening-up period* of about 15-20 minutes, (2) the *main text study* of at least 1 hour, and (3) the *closing exercise* or question in whatever time remains. This third part of the study can also lead to continuing reflection after the group disbands. If possible, never exceed the announced time for the study!

Attempt to *safeguard the participation* of all group members, both the quick ones who are not always the deepest thinkers and the slow ones who often have amazing insights to contribute. It is a good idea to proceed in this way: reading of the text, question, silent individual study, "buzz groups" (2-3 participants sitting together and exchanging their discoveries), general discussion.

For some of the studies *worksheets and visual material* are added. Photocopy these to be handed out to the participants at the appropriate point.

Study 1

1. In order to get into the time and environment of Jesus, hold up a Bible and ask group members to reflect on the questions: "What did the Bible in Jesus' time look like?", "How did young Jesus learn its content?"
2. Distribute *Worksheet A* (the summary of fictional interviews with disciples of both John the Baptist and of Jesus). Ask group members to compare the answers to the five questions. Proceed question by question with individual study, followed by buzz groups and a general discussion.
3. Tell the group about the spiritual exercise of "walking with a text". Then suggest that during the next days mem-

bers individually follow up the study by doing the exercise proposed in the last sentence of Chapter 1.

Study 2
1. Ask participants, divided into small groups, to remember and write down the seven words which, according to the four evangelists, Jesus spoke from the cross. Make sure that participants work from memory, with Bibles closed! If all the sayings are quickly remembered, ask them which evangelist reported which of the sayings.
2. Distribute *Worksheet B* (the parallel texts of part of the crucifixion accounts). For both of the following tasks allow first silent study, then buzz groups and general discussion.
   a) What are the major similarities and differences in the three accounts?
   b) Which texts from the Old Testament are quoted and alluded to? Which texts one might expect to find are *not* referred to?
3. Usually the meaning of Jesus' death is interpreted as a death for our sins, as a vicarious sacrifice. This interpretation is not found in the texts we studied. How, then, did the evangelists understand the meaning of what happened at Golgotha? What call and consolation does their testimony mean for us today?

Study 3
1. Show to the group the reproduction of the relief "Resurrection" by Friedrich Press *(Plate VI)*. What does this relief teach us about the resurrection? Silent reflection followed by general conversation.
2. Before the study session four group members have been asked to prepare reading aloud and with divided voices the passage Luke 24:1-35 (voices for a reader, a messenger, a disciple and the risen Lord). The whole text is then dramatically read and listened to once or twice. Participants respond with short spontaneous comments about

what amazed, enlightened and intrigued them while they were listening. Only then Bibles are opened to explore the Emmaus story (Luke 24:12-35). Proceed with the following three questions:

a) What is the comedy and the tragedy in this first encounter of the risen Jesus with the disciples?

b) Which are the steps leading from unbelief to belief in this story?

c) Jesus argues from the scriptures. Which Old Testament text might he have recalled?

3. The disciples recognized the risen Lord in "the breaking of the bread". Invite group members to enter, with the gestures of Jesus, into the pattern of his life, as suggested in the last paragraph of Chapter 3.

Study 4

1. Tell the group about the *Biblia Pauperum* and its way of teaching the Bible visually by showing the relationships between the Old and the New Testaments. Then hand out photocopies of the Pentecost page *(Plate VII)*. Members comment on what they see and the leader explains briefly which prophetic texts are recalled. What does this visual lesson teach us about the role of God's Spirit?

2. Biblical stories have been transmitted so that we tell them and listen to them. A good story-teller in the group has been asked beforehand to learn to tell the long story of the Spirit's meeting with Peter and Cornelius (Acts 10:1-11:18). It does not matter if the story is told with some shortenings and not always verbally, but the teller must know the different scenes by heart and tell the tale with eye-to-eye contact with group members. When the group has listened to the whole story the photocopied *Worksheet C* is distributed and silently re-read. Then proceed with the questions:

a) Who are the actors in this story? Make a list.

b) What does Peter's address teach us about the context and content of early Christian proclamation?

c) Who is being converted in this story?

3. Propose that the group begins making a visual Pentecost page for a modern *Biblia Pauperum*, as suggested in the last paragraph of Chapter 4.

Study 5

1. What does the word "heaven" mean to you? Ask the group to comment spontaneously on what they think about, feel and see when they hear the word "heaven".

2. Divide participants in two sub-groups. The first concentrates on Luke 24:44-53, the second on Acts 1:3-11. Both sub-groups examine what, according to their text, is the meaning of Ascension. Then they teach one another about what they have discovered. The main text to be studied is the difficult passage of Acts 3:17-21. The leader first explains its context (Acts 3:1-4:4). If participants have with them different Bible translations, Acts 3:17-21 is read in these different versions. Then participants individually re-read the condensed passage and transcribe its content in several short sentences. This leads to the questions:

   a) What is Christian hope according to this passage?

   b) Which other great Old and New Testament affirmations about hope come to your mind?

3. Present the statement about two different ways of facing the future (see the penultimate paragraph of Chapter 5). Are these two ways mutually exclusive? If not, how can they be combined in our daily life?

Worksheet A

John the Baptist　　　　　**Jesus of Nazareth**

1. What were John and Jesus called to do?

"The word of God came to John son of Zechariah in the wilderness. He went into all the region around the Jordan, proclaiming a baptism of repentance for the forgiveness of sins, as it is written in the book of the words of the prophet Isaiah, 'The voice of one crying out in the wilderness: Prepare the way of the Lord, make his paths straight... and all flesh shall see the salvation of God'" (3:2-6).

"He proclaimed the good news to the people" (3:18).

"Jesus, filled with the power of the Spirit, returned [from the wilderness] to Galilee... He began to teach in their synagogues and was praised by everyone" (4:14-15). After healings in Capernaum "the crowds were looking for him; and when they reached him, they wanted to prevent him from leaving them. But he said to them, 'I must proclaim the good news of the kingdom of God to the other cities also; for I was sent for this purpose'" (4:42-43).

2. What did John and Jesus say to the crowd?

"John said to the crowds that came out to be baptized by him, 'You brood of vipers! Who warned you to flee from the wrath to come? Bear fruits worthy of repentance. Do not begin to say to yourselves, 'We have Abraham as our ancestor'; for I tell you, God is able from these stones to raise up children to Abraham. Even now the ax is lying at the root of the trees; every tree therefore that does not bear good fruit is cut down and thrown into the fire'" (3:7-9).

"Whoever has two coats must share with anyone who has none; and whoever has food must do likewise" (3:11).

To tax collectors: "Collect no more than the amount prescribed for you" (3:13).

To the paralytic: "Friend, your sins are forgiven you" (5:20).

"All in the crowd were trying to touch him, for power came out from him and healed all of them.' And he said, 'Blessed are you who are poor, for yours is the kingdom of God... But woe to you who are rich, for you have received your consolation'" (6:19-24). "I say to you that listen, Love your enemies, do good to those who hate you, bless those who curse you, pray for those who abuse you. If anyone strikes you on the cheek, offer the other also; and from anyone who takes away your coat do not withhold even your shirt" (6:27-29).

After Pharisees had asked why Jesus ate and drank with tax

To soldiers: "Do not extort money from anyone by threats or false accusation, and be satisfied with your wages" (3:14).

collectors and sinners, he said, "Those who are well have no need of a physician, but those who are sick; I have come to call not the righteous but sinners to repentance" (5:30-32).

3. What did the people say about John and Jesus?

"The people were filled with expectation, and all were questioning in their hearts concerning John, whether he might be the Messiah" (3:15).

"John the Baptist has come eating no bread and drinking no wine, and you say, 'He has a demon!'" (7:33).

Jesus "has come eating and drinking, and you say, 'Look, a glutton and a drunkard, a friend of tax collectors and sinners!'" (7:34).

They say that he is "John the baptist; but others, Elijah; still others, that one of the ancient prophets has arisen". Peter said, "The Messiah of God". Jesus sternly ordered them not to say so and he announced his coming suffering (9:18-21).

4. What did John say about Jesus and Jesus about John?

"I baptize you with water; but one who is more powerful than I is coming; I am not worthy to untie the thong of his sandals. He will baptize you with the Holy Spirit and fire. His winnowing fork is in his hand, to clear his threshing floor and to gather the wheat into his granary; but the chaff he will burn with unquenchable fire" (3:16-17).

"A prophet? Yes, I tell you, and more than a prophet. This is the one about whom it is written, 'See, I am sending my messenger ahead of you, who will prepare your way before you'" [Mal. 3:1]. "I tell you, among those born of women no one is greater than John; yet the least in the kingdom of God is greater than he" (7:26-28).

5. What did John and Jesus ask about their disciples?

People said: "John's disciples, like the disciples of the Pharisees, frequently fast and pray, but your [Jesus'] disciples eat and drink" (5:33).

"Follow me" (5:27). "If any want to become my followers, let them deny themselves and take up their cross daily and follow me" (9:23).

Worksheet B

Matthew 27:45-56	Mark 15:33-41	Luke 23:44-49
(45) From noon on, darkness came over the whole land until three in the afternoon.	(33) When it was noon, darkness came over the whole land until three in the afternoon.	(44) It was now about noon, and darkness came over the whole land until three in the afternoon,
(46) And about three o'clock Jesus cried with a loud voice, "Eli, Eli, lema sabachthani?", that is, "My God, my God, why have you forsaken me?"	(34) At three o'clock Jesus cried with a loud voice, "Eloi, Eloi, lama sabachthani?" which means, "My God, my God, why have you forsaken me?"	(45) while the sun's light failed; and the curtain of the temple was torn in two.
(47) When some of the bystanders heard it, they said, "This man is calling for Elijah."	(35) When some of the bystanders heard it, they said, "Listen, he is calling for Elijah."	[(verses 36-43) "The solders also mocked him, coming up and offering him sour wine" and the word to the criminal: "Today, you will be with me in Paradise".]
(48) At once one of them ran and got a sponge, filled it with sour wine, put it on a stick, and gave it to him to drink. (49) But the other said, "Wait, let us see whether Elijah will come to save him."	(36) And someone ran, filled a sponge with sour wine, put it on a stick, and gave it to him to drink, saying, "Wait, let us see if Elijah will come to take him down."	
(50) Then Jesus cried again with a loud voice and breathed his last.	(37) Then Jesus gave a loud cry	(46) Then Jesus, crying out with a loud voice, said, "Father, into your hands I commend my spirit."
(51) At that moment the curtain of the temple was torn in two, from top to bottom. The earth shook, and the rocks were split. (51) The tombs were opened, and many bodies of the saints who had fallen asleep were raised. (53) After his resurrection they came out of the tombs and entered	and breathed his last. (38) And the curtain of the temple was torn in two, from top to bottom.	Having said this he breathed his last.

the holy city and appeared to many. (52) Now when the centurion and those with him, who were keeping watch over Jesus, saw the earthquake and what took place, they were terrified and said, "Truly, this man was God's Son!"

(39) Now, when the centurion, who stood facing him, saw that in this way he breathed his last, he said, "Truly this man was God's Son!"

(47) When the centurion saw what had taken place, he praised God and said, "Certainly this man was innocent/just."

(55) Many women were also there, looking on from a distance; they had followed Jesus from Galilee and had provided for him. (56) Among them were Mary Magdalene, and Mary the mother of James and Joseph, and the mother of the sons of Zebedee.

(40) There were also women looking on from a distance; among them were Mary Magdalene, and Mary the mother of James the younger and of Joses, and Salome. (41) These used to follow him and provided for him when he was in Galilee; and there were many other women who had come up with him to Jerusalem.

(48) And when all the crowds who had gathered there for this spectacle saw what had taken place, they returned home, beating their breasts.

(49) But all his acquaintances, including the women who had followed him from Galilee, stood at a distance, watching these things.

Worksheet C

The Spirit meets Cornelius and Peter

Scene 1 – Acts 10:1-8
Cornelius is the captain of a Roman army regiment stationed in the harbour city of Caesarea, a pious and generous man, attracted by Jewish faith, but not a circumcised convert. While he is praying an angel appears to him in a vision, asking him to send people to fetch somebody whom Cornelius does not yet know and without giving any reason. The man to be called is the apostle Peter who happens to stay in Joppa, about 50 kilometres south on the coast.

Scene 2 – Acts 10:9-16
About noon the next day Peter in Joppa is praying and gets hungry. In an ecstasy he sees the heaven opened: a sheet with all kinds of animals is handed down and a voice orders him to kill and eat. Peter refuses to do this for he has never eaten anything unclean. Three times the voice orders him to obey, adding, "What God has made clean, you must not call profane" (v.15).

Scene 3 – Acts 10:17-23a
Peter still wonders what all this might mean when the people sent to fetch him arrive. At that moment the Spirit tells him, "Look, three men are searching for you. Now get up, go down, and go with them without hesitation; for I have sent them" (v.20). They tell him about the vision of the angel which their commander received and ask him to accompany them so Cornelius might "hear what you have to say" (v.22).

Scene 4 – Acts 10:23b-29
Peter and some Jewish Christians of Joppa arrive in Caesarea where Cornelius has gathered his relatives and close friends. He receives Peter like a divine messenger. Although Peter still has reservations he enters Cornelius's home, saying to his hosts, "You yourselves know that it is unlawful for a Jew to associate with or to visit a Gentile; but God has shown me that I should not call anyone profane or unclean" (v.28). Cornelius then tells Peter his vision, ending with: "So now all of us are here in the presence of God to listen to all that the Lord has commanded you to say" (vs. 33).

Scene 5 – Acts 10:34-43
Peter's speech: (34) "I truly understand that God shows no partiality, (35) but in every nation anyone who fears him and does what is right is acceptable to him. (36) You know the message he sent to the people of Israel, preaching peace by Jesus Christ – he is Lord of all. (37) That message spread throughout Judea, beginning in Galilee after the baptism that John announced: (38) how God anointed Jesus of Nazareth

with the Holy Spirit and with power; how he went about doing good and healing all who were oppressed by the devil, for God was with him. (39) We are witnesses to all that he did both in Judea and in Jerusalem. They put him to death by hanging him on a tree; (40) but God raised him on the third day and allowed him to appear, (41) not to all the people but to us who were chosen by God as witnesses, and who ate and drank with him after he rose from the dead. (42) He commanded us to preach to the people and to testify that he is the one ordained by God as judge of the living and the dead. (43) All the prophets testify about him that everyone who believes in him receives forgiveness of sins through his name."

Scene 6 – Acts 10:44-48
(44) While Peter was still speaking, the Holy Spirit fell upon all who heard the word. (45) The circumcised believers who had come with Peter were astounded that the gift of the Holy Spirit had been poured out even on the Gentiles, (46) for they heard them speaking in tongues and extolling God. Then Peter said, (47) "Can anyone withhold the water for baptizing these people who have received the Holy Spirit just as we have?" (48) So he ordered them to be baptized in the name of Jesus Christ.

Scene 7 – Acts 11:1-18
When the apostles and the Jewish Christian congregation in Jerusalem heard what had happened there was a great stir. Peter and the eye-witnesses of the event had to go up to Jerusalem and explain why they had acted in such a shocking way, eating with uncircumcised outsiders. Peter told them of both his own and Cornelius's visions and how "the Holy Spirit fell upon them just as it had upon us at the beginning... If then God gave them the same gift that he gave us when we believed in the Lord Jesus Christ, who was I that I could hinder God?" (vv.15ff.). This, for the moment (but see Acts 15), settled the matter. "When they heard this, they were silenced. And they praised God, saying, "Then God has given even to the Gentiles the repentance that leads to life" (v.18).

Sources

Quotations

Bible quotations: The New Revised Standard Version, Nashville, TN, Thomas Nelson, 1989.

Tacitus: *The Annals of Imperial Rome*, transl. and with introduction by Michael Grant, Harmondsworth, UK, Penguin, 1956-1971.

Eusebius: *The Life of Constantine*, The Nicene and Post-Nicene Fathers, series 2, vol. 1, Grand Rapids, MI, Eerdmans, 1952-1961.

The Gospel of Peter (C. Maurer), *New Testament Apocrypha*, E. Hennecke, ed., London, Lutterworth, 1963.

Plates and figures

We have made every effort to identify the illustrations in this book and to secure the necessary permissions for reprinting. If we have erred in any way in the acknowledgments, or have unwittingly infringed any copyright, we apologise sincerely.

Plate I: Reproduced by permission of Masao Takenaka.

Plate II: © Copyright The British Museum. Reproduced by permission.

Plate III: Reproduced from Oskar Beyer, *Frühchristliche Sinnbilder und Inschriften: Lebenszeugnisse der Katakombenzeit*, Kassel, Bärenreiter-Verlag, no date.

Plate IV: Lateran Museum N171, now Vatican City.

Plate V: Museum für Kunst und Gewerbe, Hamburg. Reproduced by permission.

Plate VI: Reprinted from *Friedrich Press*, Bischöfliches Ordinariat des Bistums Meissen, Dresden, 1983.

Plate VII: Cod. pal. germ. 148. University of Heidelberg Library. Reproduced by permission.

Plate VIII: Published in *The Meaning of Icons*, Leonid Ouspensky and Vladimir Lossky, Crestwood, NY, St Vladimir's Seminary Press, 1952. Courtesy of A La Vieille Russie, New York. Photo: Helga Photo Studio.

Fig. 1: Photo Willem Van de Poll. Reproduced from *The Cambridge Bible Commentary on the New English Bible: Old Testament Illustrations*, compiled by Clifford M. Jones, Cambridge University Press, 1971.

Figs 2, 6, 7: Drawings by the author.

Fig. 3: Reproduced from *Deus Homo: Das Christusbild von seinen Ursprüngen bis zur Gegenwart*, Berlin, Evangelische Verlagsanstalt, 1973.

Fig. 4: Drawing by the author, based on an original by Jacques Briend in "La sépulture d'un crucifié", in *Bible et Terre Sainte*, vol. 133, 1971, pp. 6-18.

Fig. 5: Chludoff Psalter, Constantinople, 2.H.9. Jh., Moscow. Reproduced from *Ikonographie der christlichen Kunst*, Band 4,I: Die Kirche, Gertrud Schiller, Gütersloh, Gütersloher Verlagshaus Gerd Mohn, 1976.